⋐ ⋐ ⋐ ⋐   THE SONG OF TALIESIN

DATE DUE

GAYLORD			PRINTED IN U.S.A.

The Song of Taliesin

Tales from King Arthur's Bard

John Matthews

with illustrations by
STUART LITTLEJOHN

Quest Books
Theosophical Publishing House

Wheaton, Illinois ♦ Chennai (Madras), India

The Theosophical Society wishes to acknowledge the generous support
of the Kern Foundation in the publication of this book.

First Quest Edition 2001

The Theosophical Publishing House
P. O. Box 270
Wheaton, IL 60189-0270

Cover and text design and typesetting by Beth Hansen-Winter

Library of Congress Cataloging-in-Publication Data

Matthews, John.
The song of Taliesin: tales from King Arthur's bard / John Matthews;
with illustrations by Stuart Littlejohn. — 1st Quest ed.
      p.   cm.
Originally published: London: Aquarian Press, 1991.
ISBN 0-8356-0802-6
1. Taliesin—Literary collections.   2. Mythology, Welsh—Literary
collections.   3. Bards and bardism—Literary collections.   4. Arthurian
romances—Adaptations.   I. Title.
PR6063.A86325 S66 2001
891.6'6080351—dc21

                                                           2001031827

6   5   4   3   2   1   *   01   02   03   04   05   06

Printed in the United States of America

The Celts used their mythology, moral, heroic, magical, to give themselves a history and a system for living. Consequently, their stories inspire, thrill and enchant, while exhibiting all the worst qualities of humankind—greed, vengefulness, deviousness, violence. In myth as in life they abundantly embraced both goodness and badness and feared only boredom.

—Frank Delaney, *Legends of the Celts*

Know that my published acroamatic [esoteric] lectures can be considered as not being published, because only those who have heard me explain them will understand them.

—Aristotle to Alexander the Great

CONTENTS

ACKNOWLEDGMENTS

irst of all, my thanks must go to my life partner Caitlín, who has never ceased to offer support and encouragement despite the fact that I have been such an arch procrastinator: without you, this would never have happened, and without your work on *The Mabinogion*, it would have been ten times harder. ❧ Beyond this, my thanks go to the late Rosemary Sutcliff, who first taught me how to set the words "just so," and whose loss is deeply felt by all who love the ancient tales of the Celts. ❧ To Brenda Rosen, my editor, for recognizing the power of the stories and helping me to bring them to a second birth; to Marion Russell, the original editor of the collection, for her initial encouragement. ❧ To Jean Houston and Peggy Rubin for the wild ride in which this incarnation of the stories came to birth. ❧ To John Boorman for continuing to inspire and encourage my work in this field. ❧ To Ari Berk and Grahame Young, friends from different parts of my life, and still friends, for commenting on many of the poems and stories included here. ❧ My thanks also to Stuart Littlejohn, whose inspired pictures that so strikingly grace this volume caused many of the magical images from the stories to appear before my eyes.

NOTE ON PRONUNCIATION

WELSH NAMES

The stress comes on the penultimate syllable of a multisyllabic word, or on the first syllable of a two-syllable word. In all examples below, the stress is shown in capitals: for example, Taliesin = Tal-ee-ESS'in

All long and short vowels are roughly equivalent to Italian sung vowels except for the following:

u = i in ill or as in French tu: for example, Culhwch = KIL'hook

w = oo in look: for example, Annwn = AN'un

y = i in pin: for example, englyn = ENN'glin

y at the beginning of a word becomes like u as in but: for example, Ymerawdwr = Um-er-AWD'oor

Diphthongs follow the rules above:

eu = eye: for example, Aneurin = an-EYE'rin

ew = eoo: for example, Glewlwyd = gleoo-LOO'id

aw = ow: for example, Arawn = A-ROWN

wy = ooi: for example, Gwydion = GWID'ee-on

oe = oi: for example, Goewin = GOI'wen

Consonants are as in English except for:

c is always hard as in cake: for example, Ceridwen = Ker-ID'wen

ch = Scottish ch in loch: for example, Gwalchmai = GWALK'my

dd = th as in there, for example, Gwyddno = GWITH'no

f = v as in vet: for example, Dyfed = DUV'ed

ff = f as in faith: for example, Elffin = ELF'in

g is always hard as in get: for example, Gwynnedd = GWIN'eth ll = hl. To obtain this sound, raise the blade of the tongue to the roof of the mouth behind the tooth-ridge and aspirate huh: for example, Llefelys =Hlev-EL'is

r is slightly trilled

rh = hr: for example, Rhun = HRIN

th = th in thin (not as in there): for example, Twrch Trwyth = TOORK TROOEETH

IRISH NAMES

Some of the stories included here, in particular "Ogma: The Search for the Letters," "Amairgen's Story," and "The Fall of the Great Trees," contain names in Irish. These do not follow Welsh pronounciation rules. A selection of the main characters and words from these stories follows, with approximate pronunciations.

Aitherne = Ahern

Beil Dathi = Beel Dah'ee

Cermait = Ker'mit

Connaing Bececlach = Con'ing Bekh'lokh

Craeb Uisnig = Kreeb Ish'nig

Dairmuid mac Cerball = Dermit mak Ker'bal

Eriu = Er'a

Goibhniu = Gov'nee

Lugh = Loo'h

Sidhe = Shee

Trenfher = Tren'a

Trefuilngid Treochair = Tre-fil'nig Tre-och'er

INTRODUCTION

n 1991 I had just finished working on a historical study of native British shamanism. In the process of the ten-year period of research undertaken to complete this work, I found myself increasingly drawn to a body of stories and poems, many of them fragmentary, based on two stands of the history and mythology of the Celts. One was the vast body of material dealing with the story of the hero Arthur; the other concerned a semimythical Bard named Taliesin. ❧ Arthur, of course, is better known to us today as "King" Arthur, a medieval monarch whose legendary exploits, along with those of the Knights of the Round Table, are familiar throughout the Western world. The real Arthur was a sixth-century warrior who led a resistance movement against invaders from the north (Saxons, Angles, and Jutes) and insured himself a place in the mythical history of Britain by preserving the Celtic identity of the country for some forty years. During this time, the invaders became settlers, and the race still known as "Anglo-Saxons" came into being through intermarriage between the Northerners and the native Celts. ❧ The figure of Taliesin is much more shadowy. Almost nothing is known of him beyond what

we can discover from two sources: a sixteenth-century text in Welsh called the *Hanes* ("Life" of) *Taliesin* and seventy-seven poems in a fourteenth-century volume known as *The Book of Taliesin*, one of the Four Ancient Books of Wales collected during the late Middle Ages.

To make Taliesin's identity even more difficult to pin down, there is considerable blurring between the historical figure, who lived during the sixth century and was thus roughly contemporary to Arthur, and a more primitive, semi-mythical personality, whose name became attached to a vast body of floating lore, much of which was transmitted orally and thus had no specific author. Scholars today believe that maybe a handful of the poems that have his name attached to them may actually have been written by Taliesin. The rest are a ragbag of miscellaneous poetic fragments collected during the Middle Ages or earlier and attributed to the great Bard because of certain common magical themes found within them.

The story of Taliesin, as it is told in the fourteenth-century "Life," can be summarized as follows:

In the time of Arthur, there lived in the region of Llyn Tegid (Bala Lake) a nobleman named Tegid the Bald. His wife was named Ceridwen, and she was skilled in the magical arts. Tegid and Ceridwen had two children: One was so ugly that they called him Morfran, "Great Crow," but he came to be known as Afagddu, "Utter Darkness." The other child was a daughter, whose name was Creirwy, "Dear One." She was as fair as Morfran was dark.

Though she knew her daughter would always be loved and accepted for her beauty and gentle nature, Ceridwen feared that her son would never find his place in the world because of his hideous appearance. So, she cast about for a way to empower him with wisdom, that none might care about his looks. She resolved to boil a Cauldron of Inspiration and Wisdom according to the Books of the Fferyllt (Physicians).

The method of it was this: She was to gather certain herbs on certain days

2

and hours and put them into the cauldron, which was to be kept boiling for a year and a day, until three drops of Inspiration were obtained. For the task of maintaining the fire beneath the cauldron, Ceridwen chose an old blind man named Morda, who was led by a youth named Gwion Bach (The Little).

At the end of the year, Ceridwen stationed herself, with her son, close by the cauldron, and there she fell asleep. And while she slept, it happened that three drops flew out of the cauldron and landed on the thumb of Gwion Bach. So great was his pain that he put his thumb into his mouth and sucked it. And at once, he knew all that there was to know, and foremost of that knowledge was that Ceridwen would kill him as soon as she discovered what had happened. Because of this knowing, he fled. But the cauldron gave a great cry and cracked in two, and the waters flowed from it into a nearby stream and poisoned the water.

Ceridwen awoke, and when she saw what had occurred, her anger knew no bounds. She struck blind Morda so hard that one of his eyes fell out onto his cheek, but he said that she had injured him wrongly. Then Ceridwen knew all that had occurred and went in pursuit of Gwion, running. He was aware of her and changed himself into the semblance of a hare. She, perceiving that transformation, turned herself into the semblance of a black greyhound. He ran to a river and became a fish, but she pursued him as an otter bitch. Then he turned himself into a bird of the air, and she into a hawk. In fear for his life, he saw where a heap of winnowed wheat lay on the floor of a barn, and dropping amongst it, turned himself into one of the grains. Then Ceridwen turned herself into a black, red-crested hen and swallowed the grain of wheat, which went into her womb so that she quickened and bore Gwion for nine months.

When she gave birth to him, the child was so fair and beautiful that she could not bear to kill him or have another kill him for her. So she placed him in a leather bag and set him adrift in a coracle on the sea.

Now, at that time, there lived in the lordship of Maelgwn Gwynedd a nobleman named Gwyddno Garanhir. He had a weir on the shore of the River Conwy close to the sea. And on every May Eve, he was accustomed to take from the weir

3

salmon to the value of a hundred pounds. Gwyddno had one son who was named Elffin, a hapless youth who had nothing but evil luck. Therefore, his father told him that on this particular year, he should have all that he could find in the weir. So on May Eve, Elffin went to the weir, but when he and his servants arrived, they could see that there was not so much as a single salmon in the nets.

Then Elffin began to lament, until one of the men with him pointed out a coracle floating close by containing a leather bag. Elffin took the bag and cut a slit in it with his knife. Within, he saw a bright forehead and cried aloud, "Behold, a radiant brow" (*tal iesin*). And the child within the bag replied, "Tal-iesin shall I be called!"

Thereupon Elffin took the child up and placed it before him on the crupper of his saddle and rode for home. And as he rode, the child made a poem for him, which was "The Consolation of Elffin," and it is told that this was the first poem that Taliesin made. Elffin was filled with wonder, and he asked the child how he came to compose poetry being so young. Taliesin replied with another poem, called "The Life of Taliesin" that told how he had been present at many of the greatest events in the history of the world. For as he had been born of the Cauldron of Inspiration and Wisdom, he knew all things that were, and are, and shall be.

Now when Gwyddno heard how Elffin had failed to find any salmon in the weir, he bemoaned the ill luck of his son, but Elffin told him that he had taken from the weir something of far greater value.

"And what is that?" demanded Gwyddno.

"A Bard," replied his son.

When Gwyddno asked how that would profit him, Taliesin himself replied, "He will get more profit from me than the weir ever gave to you."

"Are you able to speak, and you so little?" demanded Gwyddno.

And Taliesin replied, "I am better able to speak than you to question me."

Whereupon Gwyddno asked him what more he had to say, and Taliesin replied with another song.

And so, Elffin gave the child to his own wife to raise, which she did most lovingly. And from that day forth, Elffin's luck turned, and he grew prosperous and was much favored by his uncle Maelgwn Gwynedd.

More adventures follow, but this part of the story defines Taliesin as not only a Bard, but also as an initiate, someone whose journey through the cycle of the elements—as hare (earth), fish (water), bird (air), and finally, the womb of Ceridwen (fire)—has taught him the secrets of time and space and given him the ability to be present at many different points of history. In these powers, he is very like the shamans of still older times. It was, in fact, this story that gave me the first clues in my own research into the survival of a shamanic tradition among the Celts practiced at least as late as Taliesin's own lifetime in the sixth century.

Behind Taliesin's story lies a vast legacy of lore and wisdom, much of it now lost. But enough has survived, in stories like those collected here, to convey the spirit and tradition of the Celts, as well as the practice of their religion. The stories you are about to read are drawn from these ancient sources. I have made the conscious effort to take them back in time to the period in which they were originally composed and to explore their deeper meanings.

Many of the stories, in their original form, are fragmentary and difficult to understand. I have therefore taken the liberty of "completing" them, drawing upon the rich heritage of Celtic myth and legend for common themes and characters. Since Taliesin is also traditionally said to have been King Arthur's Bard, I have adopted this idea throughout, making Taliesin the unofficial recorder of the life and times of *Ymerawdwr* or "Emperor" Arthur, as he is referred to in several of the oldest surviving writings of the time. I hope one day to publish an even wider exploration of this material under the collective title of *The Books of Broceliande.*

The fact that the heritage of Arthurian and related Celtic myths survives at all is due in large extent to the work of monkish scribes who collected and preserved the stories during the Middle Ages. It seemed, therefore, to be in keeping with this tradition to set the stories retold here into the framework of words written by a fictitious scribe who is presented as having collected the stories, a device that enables me to get closer to the time and place in which many of these stories were first set down and to comment upon certain aspects of them without holding up the flow of the tale or cluttering the text with too many footnotes. I trust my narrator would be grateful for my occasional interpolations to give synonyms in parentheses for obscure terms. In the process of using the little monk as my narrator, I came to "know" him almost like a friend and, at a certain point, he demanded that his own story be told. Hence the first tale in this collection.

The stories gathered here should not, then, be seen either as wholly fictional or as truly mythological, though they partake of both. Each is firmly based on existing material from medieval and earlier times, and full notes and sources will be found at the end of the book for those wishing to retrace the genesis of the stories and their relationship to each other. The poems that accompany the stories are my own, though written in the style and reflecting the content of those composed by Taliesin himself. A more detailed account of the traditions which inform all of this material will be found in my book *Taliesin: Shamanism and the Bardic Mysteries in Britain and Ireland*.[1]

It is my hope that this selection will provide a key to the secret lore of Britain, where once the Grail and the Cauldron were sought, and where the Sleeping Lord still awaits the one-who-is-to-come, who will blow the horn three times in the Cave of the Sleepers.

THE SONG OF TALIESIN

I have been
from the beginning.
I have seen
all manner of things.
My voice has been heard
upraised in song,
in the halls of kings,
in the palaces of princes,
in the houses of people,
in the groves of the Druid.
And I have sung,
let all men believe it,
before the Chair of the Sovereign,
Arthur the Blessed,
who drove all before him,
who stood at the gate of Annwn
with sword in hand
and brought forth the Hallows,
the four holy objects,
for the blessing of the Land.
I have stood on the walls
of the turning fortress.
I have dwelt three times
in the womb of the Goddess.
Bard am I,
Taliesin the singer.
I have spoken with Merlin
in his habitations of glass.

I have drunk of the awen
from the Cauldron of Inspiration,
nine nights and days
in the womb of Ceridwen.
From that day,
I have traveled the wide world.
I have stood upon the walls
of Troia the golden.
I have watched over battles
in the forefront of the host.
I have stood in the place
where the Son of Man was laid;
I have spoken to Magi
in the groves of Avaron;
I have walked all roads
between Eryri and Emmaeus;
I have heard the words
of the wisest of the wise;
I have sung to princes
in the halls of Byzantium;
I have chanted my words
before the Lords of Hosts.
Who I was
remains unknown.
In time men shall call me
Merlin and Jokannan.
Three times imprisoned
in the place of the Goddess
I still am enclosed
in the circle of the world.

In the pattern of creation
I seek my source,
in the tremendous force
of the Holy Word.
In the dreaming of choirs
of the mighty abbey,
in the halls of Lordship
and the halls of Death.
I adore the splendor
and the majesty of Fortune.
In the region of the Summer Stars
I find my beginning;
in the Circle of Abred
I observe my end.
Until that moment
in the turning spheres,
I continue my story
until called to cease.

My time will remain
in the thoughts of all,
until I enter the region
where I make my home.

1

THE SCRIBE'S STORY

I have learned to love God only slowly and with difficulty. This is part of the reason why I am setting down the things that I have gathered here, making, as it were, a heap of all I can find.[1] The story of how I met the Lord Taliesin is all a part of it and is best told here, at the beginning. ❧ Like many youngest sons I was destined for the monastery almost from birth. The fact that I grew up somewhat sickly and that I was not, therefore, like my brothers, fit material for a warrior, ensured that my father felt no regret at his decision. And perhaps I, also, felt little regret, beyond a natural sorrow at exchanging the familiar noises and smells of home for the strange, cold environment of the monastery, where it lay, a humble scattering of huts in the shelter of a small valley between green hills. ❧ The Brothers were kind, in their rough way, but I was still boy enough to feel constraint at being shut away from the world, made to work all day in the fields, milk the scrawny cow, and spend long hours on my knees in the tiny wattle and daub chapel amid the poor huts where the little community lived out its life. ❧ Yet, as I have since found to be the case with many things, there is little to which the heart and mind may not grow accustomed, given time. Not that the first years were other than hard and difficult. I was twelve when I entered the monastery, and I continued to live there for three years, during which time I proved a surprisingly apt pupil. I learned to read and write, though never well enough to work on the Great Book which was being slowly illuminated, page by glowing page, in the scriptorium. And I learned something of the properties of healing contained in certain plants.

But I was not content. Something in me longed for the freedom of the hills, for the cool winds that blew from the mountains to the north. Nor did I find the harsh dictums by which I was forced to live always palatable. And so, one day, I decided to run away.

There was nothing dramatic about the decision. It simply came to me one day that I no longer wanted to be there. Nor was it difficult. I truly believe that no one would have stopped me had I simply laid down my hoe in the midst of the fields and walked away. Yet I felt constrained, perhaps by some boyish desire for adventure, to leave at night, telling no one, having saved a few fragments of barley cake from my meager diet for a few days before.

I had no idea where I was going, but my steps led me west, then north, until the mountains were before me. I made my way deeper into their shadow, following a stream that led into a little sheltered valley among ancient rocks. At some point, the weather, which had been fair, turned first cold, then wet. There was no shelter. I walked on, head down, soaked and shivering, as night fell. I am sure that I would have died there on the mountain that night had I not stumbled in the darkness. I fell, saw stars, and felt sick and lightheaded when I tried to stand. Then I saw, through the rain, a gleam of firelight away to my left and somehow staggered towards it.

As I drew nearer, I saw that the light came from the doorway of a small hut, scarcely big enough for more than two or three men. I did not know what to do. Such a place might be inhabited by anything from an outlaw to a creature of inhuman stock. Yet, if I remained outside, I would surely be dead by morning.

Then, while I still hesitated, the door of the hut opened wider, spilling firelight out into the darkness, and a voice said, "Are you going to come in, or will you dawdle out there all night?"

With chattering teeth I moved to stand in the doorway. In front of the fire sat a man with a harp cradled in his lap. As I watched, he touched the strings, and a music so beautiful came from them that I felt at once that I wanted to go nowhere ever again, but simply to sit and listen and wait for him to play some more.

The man by the fire said, "Well, are you going to come in and shut the door, or must we both perish of the cold?" I stepped across the threshold, closed the door on the cold and wet and dark, and entered upon the greatest adventure of my life.

That was the first time that I laid eyes upon the Lord Taliesin, Primary Chief Poet of the Island of the Mighty. Later, crouched by the fire, having consumed a bowl of hot broth, which he gave me, I studied him. He was tall, very sparely built, with a lined face. I thought him somehow old, though his hair was black and his back straight. His face seemed cast in a sardonic mode, but there were lines of sorrow—even of suffering—about his mouth. His eyes were green, rather cold, I thought, and neither friendly nor unfriendly.

After his first words to me, he did not speak again, handing the bowl of broth to me and returning at once to silent contemplation. I was used enough to silence after three years in the monastery and knew better than to interrupt. The warmth of the fire and the hot food, after the cold and wetness of the night, soon took effect. My head fell forward, and I slept where I sat.

Later, cramps woke me, and I found that I had been covered by a blanket. The fire had died down to a red heap of ashes, by which dim glow I saw that my host appeared hardly to have moved from the position in which I first saw him. He had laid aside the harp and sat with his knees drawn up to his chin, a position I was to see him adopt often in later years.

As quietly as I could, I eased my position and found that my host's eyes were upon me. Leaning forward suddenly, he poked at the gleeds of the fire. By the small flare of light thus afforded, he seemed to study me. Then he laughed quietly.

"Is it not strange that we should meet, here of all places?"

I shook my head dumbly.

"Well, perhaps not." He sighed and, reaching out, touched the harp where it lay close to hand. A thread of sound whispered in the little hut. "Sleep now," he said, and I felt my eyes close as if in answer to a command.

I awoke to pale, watery sunlight shining in through the open door of the hut. The fire had been freshly laid, and a small cauldron of food was simmering over it. My host stood by the door, looking out at the morning. As I stirred, he turned to look at me but did not speak. He remained silent while we broke our fast; then, as I hungrily devoured the very last scrap, he took up the harp and began to play.

Never had I heard such sounds. I was entranced as completely as if some spirit of the woodland or the mountain had laid a spell upon me. After a while, he began to chant words that twined about the music in bright threads. The words have never left me, and though they seem as strange to me now as they did then, I can remember them as well as if they were being sung now, though it is many years since the events of which I write.

> *I feel my way into the rock.*
> *I finger the dark holes of its brain.*
> *My hands encounter the dark.*
> *My eyes see with the sight of the rock.*
> *I breathe out with the breath of the rock.*
> *My fingers the wind touches, and my feet the sea washes.*
> *My thought lies in the head of the rock—*
> *Tintagel, gripping the White Brow.*
> *My sweat runs in streams down the face of rock.*
> *I mingle with the sea-salt and sea-mist.*

I blow out on the wind's back.
The sky swallows my heart.
I beat with the tick of the beating world.
I beat.
The wind shakes my hair.
The sand forms itself to a pattern:
An Iron Crown, spiked and spurred.
My fingers forget they are fingers.
My body forgets all it has remembered.
I learn the secret of the birth of rock.
A seabird without wings I am swept
Into the sky—through the sky.
Air rocks my wings.
In the cave my fingers and feet
Release rock. Strands of hair
Twist in water and in air.

He finished, and we both sat in silence for an age. Then the poet looked at me again and said, not unkindly, "You are too early, little monk; go home now."

That was all he said to me, yet I got up like one in a dream, went out of the door, and followed the path down from the hut and back along the road by which I had come. At the monastery, the Abbot was not unkind; he must have been used to boys my age running away and clearly expected me to return. I said nothing, either then or later, about my encounter with the poet. But the memory of that meeting, and the memory of the strange and wonderful song, remained with me.

I did not try to run away again, but settled to the round of work and prayer in the monastery. The years passed, and we heard rumors of the great events in the world outside, of the coming of the Great King and of the Fellowship he gathered about him whose aim was to put right the wrongs that weakened the land of Britain. We heard, also, of Merlin, whom many believed to be a devil's son, or even a follower of the terrible old Druids whom the Romans had all but destroyed long ago, but who were rumored to be still hidden in certain parts of the land. And we heard of Taliesin, the King's Poet, the mightiest Bard in all of Britain and a man both feared and loved. Strange stories were told of him: that he had been initiated into pagan mysteries even older than those of the Druids; that he could sing a whole room full of fierce fighting men to sleep; that (even more darkly) he could change his shape at will.

Of course, no one really believed these things, except perhaps sometimes in the half-light of an evening, or when strange noises came out of the darkness as we knelt at our prayers in the little chapel.

In this time, I came to know more of the Most High God and of his gentle Son and to accept their way as the one and only truth. My life was wholly bound and absorbed by the daily pattern of our community, and even the memory of my brief escape into the world faded somewhat.

Then the day came when I was sent on an errand. I was to lead the party of Brothers taking the Great Book, finished at last, to the Mother Church of our order at Carlisle, where the head of our order was also to be found. It was a long and fearful journey for all of us, who had almost without exception never been beyond the confines of the valley in which our monastery stood. But the Most High protected us, and we arrived with our precious burden unharmed.

The city was full of people, more than most of us had ever seen in one place at one time. We learned that this was in part because the Great King, with all his court, was there as well.

That same day we learned that the King and some of his retinue were to go outside the city to hunt game in the great forest of Inglewood, which lay to the south. As chance would have it, their route took them past the Holy House where our party was residing during our stay in the city. Curiosity got the best of me when I heard cheering outside, and I went to the window to watch the great ones ride past.

There, I saw, for the first and only time, the Great King himself, the

Ymerawdwr Arthur. He was as strong and stern as I had been told, though I also saw that he suffered in some way that I could not fathom. There was gray in his hair already, though he could not have seen above thirty-five summers. But it was not upon him that my eyes rested for the longest time, but the man who rode at his side. Tall, sparely built, with dark hair bound back in a fillet of bronze, his cold green eyes glancing this way and that as he rode, as though searching for something. He had not changed at all in the years since our meeting in the little hut in the mountains. He seemed neither older nor younger, though the lines were perhaps a little more deeply graven around his mouth than before.

Our eyes met for a moment that seemed to last forever, and I heard, inside my head, as clearly as if he had spoken the words into my ear, "Not yet, little monk, but soon." Then the company was past, and I stood alone, suddenly shivering as though with cold, though the day, as I remember it, was hot.

I turned to the Brother who stood next to me and asked who the man was who rode at the High King's side. He made the sign of the Cross before answering. "That is Taliesin, the King's Bard. It is best you do not even look at him, for he is surely in league with the devil."

I looked hastily away, but in my heart I was certain—as indeed I am today—that there was nothing evil in the poet, for all his strange and sometimes fearful ways.

I returned to the monastery with my Brothers and tried to settle again to the rhythm of the community. But the face of the Lord Taliesin was never far from my mind, and his words rang often in my thoughts when I should have been thinking of God.

Five more years passed. Then news came of fighting away in the south and of the disappearance of the Great King. Rumors filled the Land, flying hither and yon. We heard how there was a great battle between the Lord Arthur and his own son Mordred, who men said was the offspring of unholy incest with his sister, the witch Morgain. Many of the High King's Fellowship fell there, and many other good men. The Brothers were on their knees all night long praying for the souls of the dead.

But I felt something more than sorrow for the ending of what had been a great and mighty dream. The thought of the Lord Taliesin filled my mind day and night. None mentioned his name, and I dared not ask for fear of being thought ungodly.

Then one night I awoke from sleep suddenly, as though a hand had been laid on my shoulder. It was utterly dark and silent in the dormitory where I lay, save for the snores of one of the Brothers. I rose and made my way outside. Something made me look up at the heavens, and I saw a sky ablaze with stars, brighter than I ever remembered seeing them. Briefly, I thought I saw a shadow wing its way among them. I shivered, not from the chill of the night alone, and went back to my cot, determined upon a course of action that I saw as clearly as though I had been thinking of it for a long time—as indeed, perhaps, I had.

Next day I sought out the Abbot, a different man to the old one who had been there when I entered the monastery. I told him that I was leaving, perhaps forever; and though he questioned me, I gave no reason for my decision, only assuring him that I had suffered no lapse of faith. He must have seen the determination in me, for he made no attempt to argue against my decision. Next morning, I left the little community for the last time and set out for the mountains to the north.

A day later, I found myself once again on the path that led to the hut where I had spent so memorable a night many years before. I found that I remembered the way as clearly as if my previous visit had been only a day earlier. The hut was much as I remembered it, crouching back against the face of a sheer cliff, a little more weather-beaten, but otherwise sound. The door stood open, and as I approached across the grassy table of earth, I heard a thread of music that I remembered well. Still I hesitated, finding myself suddenly shy. Why had I come, and what sort of welcome would I find?

Then the voice of the poet came from within, "Are you going to come in or stand out there all day?" I went inside and found him seated, much as before, the harp cradled in his arms. The years had passed him by, while I had grown to manhood and into middle years.

I sat down before him and looked into those unfathomable eyes. After a moment, he touched the strings of the harp briefly. Then he said, "It is time now, little monk. We have much to do."

That was all there ever was between us by way of asking or acceptance of the task I undertook. Every day thereafter I spent several hours in the company of the poet while he told me story after story, which I attempted to write down, either while he spoke or afterwards from memory. It was as though he was unburdening himself of a great weight that he had carried with him for many years—longer indeed than he could remember. He scarcely ever spoke of the days he had spent with the High King, and I now believe that it was during this time that he wrote the great chronicle of those times, which I discovered after his departure.

I learned much from him that was both strange and fearful, though I still believe that there is nothing of evil in his works. Above all, he spoke to me of the great forest of Broceliande, which seemed at times to extend over the greater part of the Land, though whether in fact or fancy I cannot say. He said, once, that the stories of the Wood were as numerous as leaves on its trees. I still do not know if he told me all the stories that he knew; I believe not. But each one had something to teach, some piece of lore and wisdom from the days before the message of the Lord Christ came to Britain.

As you read these things, you may, if you desire it, imagine the two of us, the Lord Taliesin and myself, seated in the little hut on the mountainside, he speaking, sometimes rapidly, sometimes with long pauses as though he sought far back into his memory to recollect some detail of the story, myself crouched over a makeshift writing desk, struggling to recall the exact words and to set them down so that they might be read by all men when the Land was at peace again.

For most of that year we labored. It seemed at times as though my master— for such always I thought of him—was hastening to conclude the work we did before some event overtook him. I believe now that he was preparing to leave even as he waited for me. Then, one morning, I awoke to find him gone. Believing he had simply stepped out to take the morning air, or to catch something for the pot, I sharpened my quill and waited. But the morning passed into afternoon, and there was no sign of him. I began to believe that he had gone for good, and gradually, as the days passed, I knew that my fears were well founded. Taliesin had gone, whither I knew not. He had made no farewells any more than he had spoken a greeting to me. Yet I felt no anger at this. I had come to know him well enough by then to understand that such was his way.

I remained in the little hut for several more months, adding details to the stories I had already written, making fair copies of others. Then, one day, a boy came to the hut. He was starving and ill, and I took him in, nursing him slowly back to health. When he was better, he seemed reluctant to leave, and so together we built a lean-to shelter against the side of the hut, and there he stayed. I began to teach him to read and write and the beginnings of the way of the Lord Christ.

He was only the first of many who seemed to know that safety lay in the little shallow valley among the mountains. Soon there were ten living there, men and women both and, in time, a small community was established. One winter I grew ill and was nursed back to health by those whom I had helped. They insisted that I must have a better place to live and built me a new hut close to the old one. It was while I was clearing out the hut that had belonged to my master that I found a small, intricately carved box hidden in a niche of the rock against which the hut had been built. In it I found a kind of farewell, the great legacy of the Lord Taliesin's writing—his account of the days of the High King Arthur and the Fellowship, of the quest for the Holy Cup, and of the fate that overtook them all. I learned, too, even more of the story of the forest, Broceliande, the World Wood, in whose mazes the poet had walked and watched and observed all that passed in that strange and wondrous time.

In the last few years, as I have grown older, I have undertaken the task, which I have found by no means easy, of placing all that he wrote, or instructed me to write, in order, so that they may be properly read and studied in future time, when, I pray God, the Land is more settled. There are those who would destroy the works of my master, thinking them heretical or dangerous; yet I find that despite certain heathenish ideas, he strove always to tell the truth as he saw it, and while there is much that I myself find amazing or intractable of belief, yet even here I see no actual evil, nothing to hinder the prayers I offer up daily to my Lord Christ for his soul. As to whether he is dead or living, I know not, but I believe that I shall not meet with him again in this life.

As to the truth or otherwise of the stories, I remember clearly the words of their author, regarding his works: "Though I may seem to speak as one who was present, there are times when I was not. I tell what is there to be told, in whatever words are given me by the *awen* (inspiration)." This I take to mean that by some means no longer understood, he was able to observe events at which he was not always present in the flesh. How this may be accomplished is not my concern; I record it simply for the interest of those who delight in such matters, or who seek better to understand the works of my Lord Taliesin. Beyond this, I have dared to set my own words down in this place, to tell my own story of my fateful meeting with the Primary Chief Bard of the Island of Britain. Lest those who read this think me too bold, I will but say that I do so in humility and only with the purpose of explicating the darker corners of my master's writings. For the rest, the reader must judge what is true or not.

It seems more than strange to me now that I lived through the age of Arthur, yet knew almost nothing of the great events that took place in the world beyond the monastery in the sheltered valley. Yet I see, too, that we were left in peace throughout those years because the Ymerawdwr and his Fellowship were there, guarding the Island of the Mighty against many evils, until it was breached from within.

I have kept all of Taliesin's writings with me here, but now that I grow old, I have begun to think how best to dispose of them so that they will remain safe. There are many who would destroy these writings if they could, and still others who would use them for their own ends. Therefore I must hide them all, until a better time comes. I give daily thanks to the Most High God for the brief fellowship of the Lord Taliesin, whom I now believe to have been the wisest man alive in these troubled times. I pray that others may one day read what I have written and understand, as I have done, the value of what is here.

THE PLANETARY SPHERES

Taliesin heard the music of the spheres.
He spoke from age to age,
Seeing how each life was marked
By its place in the Zodiac of Time.
Under the stars of light he found
The dwelling place of the gods.
Fallen or dead, he looked
Among them for the King's shadow
Stretching from Aquarius to Mars.
The poet traced his destiny
From the double-birth of Gemini
To the rise of Lunar West.

2

THE CAULDRON-BORN

This account, which I set down first of all, was not among those told to me by my master. I found it among the great mass of documents he left behind. It bears all the marks of hurried composition and seems to have been written long ago. I cannot repress a shudder as I read it—not only for its heathenish content, but for the vision it contains. But because I take it to be true, in whatever fashion, I set it down with the rest.

It is not the vow of secrecy that prevents the initiate from revealing what he has learned. Nor is it a desire to keep the truth to himself. What he sees is TRUTH itself, the whole truth, and that is sometimes so terrible that he dare not speak of it, even to himself. So it is not my solemn vow that I am breaking by telling you this; it is fear I overcome. ❧ I am Taliesin and I am a Poet. As such I know the power of words—the building of one syllable upon another; the placing of the words in certain order so that they make a single, incontestable truth. ❧ Once, before all this, I had another name. I was called Gwion, and I was the servant of the Old One. No job too dirty or too mean for Gwion, whether it was cleaning up after her half-wit son, Afagddu, or stirring the black pot that hung over the fire when she was brewing up some new mischief to plague the world. I used to believe all the evils of the world came out of that cauldron; now I know that only truth is to be found inside its cold rim—truth which, acceptable or not, is still terrible to behold. Yet truth has no quality of good or evil; it is simply there, passionless like a clear glass or a still pool between white trees.

One day the Old One came into the hut where she kept her few scrawny pigs, her cauldron, and me, cuffed me about the head, and ordered me to prepare a fire and set up the cauldron for some new work she intended to begin. "So waste no time, youth, or you will see how I reward you!"

Such expressions of love I was well acquainted with and knew better than to ignore. I struggled to mount the huge black pot onto its tripod and then set about laying a fire. I filled the cauldron with water as I had been taught and got as far out of the way as I could, crouching in the corner of the hut until I was needed again.

The Old One took five days to gather all the ingredients necessary for her new potion, and I had to keep the cauldron simmering while she went out to get them. At the end of nine days, a stinking, viscous fluid filled the pot, and the Old One left me again with strict instructions not to let the mixture boil over or do anything else to it. "And don't touch any, or you'll regret it," she said, though why she should think I might want to do so was a mystery to me.

There was certainly no intention in me to disobey. I had felt the wrath of Herself before, knew that her shapely white hands could cause greater torment than one would believe possible of anyone—let alone someone as beautiful as she, with her white, white skin and black hair. But I must have put too much kindling under the cauldron, because it began to bubble suddenly, and as I went to dampen it down, several bubbles burst, and some drops—there may have been three—splashed onto my hand.

They were scalding hot, and I yelped with the pain and put my hand to my mouth to suck it. Immediately the world turned around me, and I fell into a dark,

CERIDWEN

roaring place where sound and sensation were too great to bear, and where I, Gwion, became lost, never to return.

And what I saw there is what I must tell, for the drink was the drink of initiation, brewed for the Old One's monstrous son. In its black bile I tasted and saw all the sickness and all the waste of the world and the long, slow poison of the soul of humankind. And there, too, I saw the dawn of hope, the coming of one whose presence would change the world for all time—aye, even to its very end—though I knew naught of this then, nor for long after.

Sensations: Pain. Fear. Horror. Such fear as wraps one in cold like a mist, nebulous, nameless, and unformed, but real as the pain of birth and dying. Pain dragged me down into a bottomless dark where meaning no longer held good

27

and where the identity that made me Gwion left its existence behind. Horror of darkness, void, negative terror that spells an end to life, to hope, to belief in anything, swept through me.

Then, light. A bursting forth of such brilliance that to look upon it unprepared was to be blinded. I was not so prepared, but I had sense enough to look away, to study it in the reflections of the eye—a half-light and a half-truth were all I could bear.

Faces swam towards me out of the light. Some smiled. Some frowned. I recognized none of them. I saw men in agony, men transformed, men who wept and laughed at life. And I saw women of unearthly beauty, whose appearance was such that I grew afraid for my very soul and tried to look away.

Then I heard voices. Calling out. Screaming. Shouting. The sounds of battle and love, of birth and death, of agony and pleasure, of joy and fear. I closed my light-seared eyes and tried to shut out the sounds. But nothing would avail, and I found that only by opening myself to everything, could I, somehow, bear it. I let myself be filled up with sound and light and movement—all these sensations set forth in a dimension of understanding that made me aware of them to a degree almost impossible to bear.

So things stood. But for a moment only. For the time it takes to blink an eye, all knowledge and understanding were mine. And, as I entered this realm of infinite possibilities, I knew that the Old One was aware of me and of what had occurred. For now I shared a part of her knowledge and her life.

She was coming after me.

I fled through a timeless landscape: hill, river, and wood flowing past and around me as though they had no substance, and I waded in them. All the time I felt the presence of the Old One, like a shadow flying over the earth, closer and closer behind.

To aid my escape, I put on the gloves and ears of the hare and sped with the hare's speed, but I knew that she followed me still with the tongue and teeth of the greyhound and ran as fast as I. So I donned the feet and tail of the otter and sped through a watery world where startled fish broke on either side of my head. But as a hound, the Old One sniffed my passage and came after me, so that I was forced to take the wings of the bird. Even there she came, a hawk striking at my feathered back. And so at last, to elude her I became a grain of wheat in a heap of chaff. But I knew, with my strange new awareness, that I was caught. And sure enough, the Old One took me in her hen's beak and swallowed me down. Then she became herself, and I found myself asleep in the fluid darkness of her womb. In this darkness I began to dream.

Of a shadow that gave forth light, showing me a desolate place where no grass grew, where the trees were leafless and the ground cracked and dry. Then, into that waste, came a tendril of green that sent forth shoots, until a spider web of green lay across the dead earth . . .

Of a man who struggled all his life against terrible odds, who tried to fight the inexorable force of fate and who, at death, smiled not with the joy of release, but with malicious pleasure that others would suffer as he had suffered . . .

Of a great building that reached higher and higher into the sky towards God, but had its roots in sand. Below the sand, black stinking mud. The building falling, crushing men. One—a boy only—had worked with skill and love to fashion a figure onto the stone that killed him . . .

Of a world, this world, and a cloud stretching forth to cover it, threatening. Faces appearing in the cloud, lit with strange lights. Beautiful faces. Cruel faces. Faces smooth and dark with unspoken desires . . .

✦

Of blood, raining from the sky . . .

✦

Of water, bubbling from a broken fountain rim . . .

✦

Of a man, descending on a spiral stair, deeper and deeper below the world of light and day. In his hand, a flickering lantern that showed only walls slimed with fungus. At the bottom of the shaft, a room deep in human filth, and crouching in it, an old blind woman, deathless and hideous, obscene, crouching and crouching, demanding that he kiss her flayed face and running sores. Sucking the life from him like a terrible spider . . .

✦

Of earth herself: the great womb, teeming with all these images and more, far more than I can tell. Blind and dark, I crawled through the hot passageways within her vast bulk, my hands encountering nameless things that moved beneath me . . .

✦

Then suddenly an absence of darkness into which I stumbled, blind. At first no difference, nothing I could name as light. But a warm hand, full of life, lifting me up; wings, or petals, enfolding me; and a warmth that was also a voice, neither male nor female, somehow inside my head, uttering words that were instantly transformed into images. An experience of the pains of creation, containing dark as well as light—tenderness and purity invoked.

All these things swirling together. And more. And yet more. And yet more still—all different, all the same, man and woman the same, death and birth the same. A great conjoining. A birth. My own birth cry in the heavens as I fell from the womb of the Old One into the light of the world whose soul I had seen die and be reborn . . .

And waking, shivering, on the mountainside, the cup still clutched in my numb fingers, the spiraling maze stilling at last beneath my gaze . . .[1]

It is these things which seal the lips of the initiate, not the promise made at the door to the Mysteries. I, Taliesin, once Gwion, now reborn, Cauldron-born of the Old One whose ways have no more terror for me, born of the drink all must drink, know these things.

TALIESIN'S CREED

In the rock, alive,
I would be hewn from it
Like a dream of stone—
Like Merlin, my brother,
In the hidden place.

A feather in bright air
I drift in memory's disguise,
Shadowy as sunlight
Shaped by sea.
Half in, half out,
I am reborn.

I am in the stone
I am in the wood
I am in the sun
I am in the dancing
I am in all things—

This is my freedom
This my strength
This my journeying
This my discovery
This shaped my self!

3

THE JOURNEY TO DEGANWY

You will have heard the story of how I came ashore at Gwyddno's weir and became Bard and tutor to his son Elffin.[1] What happened after that needs to be told also, for it is part of the pattern of the story that has been mine to pursue—whether through the Forest of Broceliande or through the forest in my head, I leave it to others to decide.

This is the first mention I find among the papers that my master left to my care of the great forest, which he usually refers to simply as "The Wood." It seems that he deemed this place to be of great importance to him and felt that, in some mysterious fashion, it affected his life and that of the Ymerawdwr Arthur. ❧ I myself may not comment upon these things, but I believe that the words my master wrote show that he saw clearly where others saw only shadows.

I found life at Gwyddno's court comfortable enough, though dull, after the initiation of the Cauldron, which I deemed had prepared me for greater things. But I soon learned that a shadow lay upon the household of Elffin and his father and that the shadow bore a name—Maelgwn Gwynedd.

Maelgwn—what an evil smirch his name has left upon the Land of Britain! He fought his way to the lordship of all Gwynedd by murder and trickery, leaving more than one good man dead in his wake. A grandson of old Cunedda himself, he had good claim to half the lands of the Cymry. But his dark ways and restless temper betrayed him at every turn, so that instead of following his father Catawallawn Longhand in the lordship of Gwynedd, when Longhand died in battle at Penrhiaidd, the diadem went to Cunedda's other son, Ewein Whitetooth. The young Maelgwn found himself in a monastery, learning to recite the scriptures and write his name in Latin from no lesser teacher than old St. Illtud himself, a grim prelate if ever there was one. There, as fate would have it, he began a friendship with another pupil, Gildas, who many years later, in his famous *Ruin of the Britons*, was to write of his one-time friend that he was "the worst of all the tyrants of Britain, the most evil, sinful man, a murderer and a wolf in sheep's clothing," from which you may see the effect that Maelgwn had upon even those who once loved him.

When he had been at the monastery only a year, Maelgwn perpetrated a crime of such violence and duplicity against the monks that he was forced to leave, earning himself the undying hatred of Gildas, who despite his famous vitriolic attacks on various of the royal families of Britain, was not an unfair man. Certainly his comments on men such as Constantine, Aurelius Caninus, and the old wolf Vortipore are just after their own lights.

As to Maelgwn's crime, I believe that he took a lover from amongst the brethren, an occurrence of no great rarity in such circumstances, as you will know, little monk. Anyway, the love turned sour, and the youth was found dead, whether killed by Maelgwn himself or by his own hand, who can say.

Here my master is harsh to a degree upon the life of the Brothers. Though the unnatural lust of which he speaks is not unknown, I myself saw none of it in

MÆLGWN GWYNEDD

my own monastery. The hard and relentless regime of labor leaves little time or desire
for such things.

Many more dark stories are told of Maelgwn, but as ever, I will try to set
straight the record from my knowledge of things that took place within the confines of the Wood. It is said, for example, that Maelgwn became lord of Powys by
murdering his uncle Whitetooth. That is only half the truth. There is little doubt
that Maelgwn had the old king removed, but there is more to the story than this.

The lands of Gwynedd and those of Cantr'e Gwaelod, which were already
ruled over by Gwyddno Garanhir at the time of which I speak, were bordered on
one side by the sea. From most distant times, there existed an understanding
between the Kings of Gwynedd and the Lady of the Sea that certain dues must be
paid in order that the Land should not be overwhelmed by the hungry water.
Thus every year the kings of these two provinces performed a ceremony whereby

they pledged themselves to the sea like husbands to a bride. I tell elsewhere what happened when Gwyddno turned against this practice.[2] For the moment, it is enough to say that Maelgwn saw a way to assure his own right to his uncle's lands by allowing the sea to decide in his favor.

This was the way of it.

Maelgwn called together the five lordlings who might be said to have a claim upon the lands of Ewein Whitetooth and placed his own claims before them. Then, before they could protest their own rights, he suggested that the Lady of the Sea herself should decide among them. The way this was to be done was as follows: All six chieftains, including Maelgwn, were to be carried in six chairs to the edge of the sea and there left to await the incoming tide. He who remained longest in his place was to be the new lord of Gwynedd.

How could they refuse? To do so would have been to deny the power of the Goddess who had ruled their lives for centuries. The place chosen was a wide stretch of sand at the mouth of Afon Dyfi, which was completely covered at high tide. Here the lords were carried in their chairs of state, and there they sat, while at a respectful distance, the people of Gwynedd stood and watched and waited.

Gradually the tide rose, and the lords began to look nervously at each other. First it lapped at their feet; then it covered them, rising slowly first to calves and then knees and finally to waist level. The heavy chairs began to settle in the sands or to rock a little with the incoming swirl of the tide.

But not so Maelgwn's. He sat serenely in his chair, which lifted gently off the sands and, as the tide rose, rose with it, until it was floating evenly on the sea itself. The other lords were discomfited, and the people acclaimed Maelgwn as their lord. What they did not know was that he had sought the magical aid of old Afallach himself, whose daughter Gwallwenn Maelgwn already loved, though he was not to marry her for many years after, and that in a dark and treacherous way.[3]

Thus it was that this stretch of coast became known as Traeth Maelgwn, Maelgwn's Sands, and he became lord of Gwynedd through a trick, which was to go unpunished for many years. I do not know why the Goddess permitted this injustice, any more than I know why she chose to take back Llacheu[4] and Arthur, son and father, but thus it was.

Once he was established, Maelgwn looked at once to Sanant, the sister of Brocfael, Lord of Powys, for a wife. In this way he established ties between the two lordships, which he no doubt intended to bring under his own sway in due time.

Thus matters stood when I first came to the court of Gwyddno. Maelgwn was an uncomfortable neighbor, forever sending his men on careless raids that somehow strayed onto Gwyddno's lands. Not that the old warrior failed to defend himself. He was assured in his place and had the support of neighboring lords who were as sick of Maelgwn as he was. And so an uneasy peace existed between them, which allowed people from Gwyddno's court to visit that of his neighbor at Deganwy, which was, I will confess, both rich and splendid. Maelgwn maintained himself well, with a retinue of Bards, including the famous Hennin Fardd,[5] and a strong Druid presence.

Elffin used often to visit there, being less perspicacious than his father and liking to spend time drinking and gaming with the more polished youth of Gwynedd's court. Unfortunately, this habit was to get him in trouble, as well as to give Maelgwn the opportunity of making Gwyddno and his family look foolish. This was the way of it.

One day Elffin was sitting with some of his friends who numbered themselves among the sycophants of Maelgwn, when talk came round to the subject, first, of the qualities of the court Bards, and second of the qualities—beauty, chastity, and so forth—of their Lords' wives. Of course the men of Deganwy immediately sang the praises of Maelgwn's Bards and of his wife Sanant, who was, by all accounts, both fair and gentle and no match for her husband. But Elffin made a mistake. He mentioned myself and his own wife, Elaint, who he claimed was more beautiful and talented and chaste even than Sanant. Of course, his words were reported to Maelgwn within the hour, and the Lord of Gwynedd, with a fine show of rage, had Elffin incarcerated while he "investigated the truth of these allegations."

Poor Elffin. He had meant no harm. It was simply the age-old pride of his race that had spoken out. And he was, indeed, genuinely fond of Elaint. Now he found himself in dire straits, locked up, while Maelgwn began his "investigation."

Now the way Maelgwn went about discrediting Elffin, and through him, Gwyddno, was to send his son Rhun to find out firsthand whether Elaint was more beautiful and chaste than Sanant. Rhun was little better than his father, a blustering, boorish womanizer, who claimed to have bedded more women at court than anyone else.

Well, he put on his finest clothes and set out for Gwyddno's hall. But he had reckoned without Elffin's Bard. For I was Gwion no longer, but Taliesin, and I was eager to try my new found abilities. So I sought out Elaint and told her what had occurred. She wasted no time asking how I knew. Facing me in the little sunny *grianan* (sun-house) where she spent much of her time, she anxiously questioned me as to what course of action she should follow. She was all for running to Gwyddno, but I dissuaded her from this course, knowing that this was exactly what Maelgwn hoped for—the beginning of a quarrel that he would soon turn into a war. I put an alternate plan to Elaint, and she agreed to try my way first, for she could see that thus the tables might well be turned upon Elffin's captor.

Rhun duly arrived and was made welcome. The laws of hospitality required that he be treated as an honored guest, though indeed, there were few there who liked him any more than they liked Maelgwn. He, of course, took the first opportunity that arose to pay his respects to the wife of his "good friend" Elffin.

He was shown into her private room, where she sat at her sewing, waited upon by her maid. What foolish Rhun did not know was that I had instructed Elaint to change places with the maid. She who sat now at the table was the maid, while her mistress looked to her needs like a serving woman.

Rhun began to ply his way with flattery and winning words. The Mistress/ Maid listened, bridling and tossing her head as though all that he said was just what she liked to hear. Rhun called for beer; the Mistress/Maid drank. Rhun flattered her some more; she grew coy and simpering. At length her head sank on her arms, and a small snore escaped her. Rhun laughed and, taking out his knife, cut the little finger, which bore a splendid ring, from her right hand. The woman scarcely stirred.

Rhun left quietly, and Elaint hurried to bind up the poor woman's injured hand. I waited, knowing what was to happen next.

Rhun returned jubilant to his father, displaying his grisly trophy. Elffin was summoned and stood before Maelgwn, who showed him the finger with the ring upon it. Rhun explained that he had come by it after dishonoring Elffin's wife. Elffin merely looked at the finger in a thoughtful kind of way.

"Well," he said, "whoever it was your son was with, it was not my wife. Firstly, though I recognize the ring as hers, it would scarcely stay upon her thumb, whereas here it is tightly fitted over a little finger. Secondly, my wife pares her nails every week. This finger has not been pared for a month and, as you see, it has recently kneaded dough. Elaint has not made bread in my house since we were married."

Maelgwn's anger was great. He almost knocked Rhun to the ground in his fury, while Elffin was dragged away to confinement again, "until such time as the worth of your Bard is proved!"

This also I had foreseen and was prepared for it. While I waited for the time to be right for my own journey to Deganwy, I made a new song, which I sang to Elaint to soothe her fears for the life of Elffin.

> *I'll set out on foot.*
> *To the gate I'll come.*
> *I'll enter the hall.*
> *My song I'll sing.*
> *My verse I'll proclaim*
> *In the presence of the Chief.*
> *The Bards I'll cast down*
> *And chains I'll break—*

Elffin I'll set at liberty.
When contention arises
In the presence of chieftains,
And Bards are summoned
To sing faithful harmony—
With magician's skills
And Druid wisdom
In the court there'll be
Some cunning tricks.
No grace or blessing
On Maelgwn Gwynedd,
For this fearful wrong
And ingenious cruelty.
Vengeance shall end it,
On Maelgwn and Rhun.
May his life be short,
May his lands be wasted,
May his exile be long—
This upon you, Maelgwn Gwynedd!

Having delivered myself of this song, I set out, reaching Deganwy as night was falling. I made my way to the great hall and, slipping inside unnoticed, took up a position in a dark corner. The evening feast was already under way, and in a while, I saw a group of Bards enter and make their way to the cleared space by the hearth. Foremost was Hennin Fardd himself. As they passed, I pouted my lips and played on them with my fingers in such a way as to form a sound something like "blerwm, blerwm." Then I watched as Maelgwn called for a praise song, and the hall fell silent.

Hennin Fardd stepped forward and signed to his harper to begin playing. Like many of the effete court Bards, he no longer played his own music, but sang to accompaniment. This time, however, I was there, and all that came from his mouth was a sound something like "blerwm, blerwm."

The whole court went rigid from shock. Maelgwn's mouth dropped open and then color rose to his cheeks. Again the desperate Bard tried to begin his song, but all that would come forth was the sound of "blerwm, blerwm." Maelgwn, unable to restrain himself any longer, jumped up, and crossing the space between them, felled the stupefied Bard with a single blow. The shock loosened his tongue, and he began to babble apologies. Then, abruptly, he fell silent and turned to look in my direction. He had felt my presence, for he was, after all, an initiate himself.

"That is the cause of this mockery," he cried, pointing a trembling finger at the corner where I sat. "Come forth, imp."

I stood up and walked into the light of the smoky torches. I had to hold onto myself to avoid shaking with helpless laughter and did so only by remembering the reason for my coming there. I stopped before Maelgwn, who looked me up and down with shrewd eyes. He saw that there was more to this whole business than was at once apparent. At length, he demanded, "Who are you?"

"I am Elffin's Bard."

A ripple of sound spread behind me through the hall. Maelgwn's eyes narrowed. He was a tall man, with black hair worn long and tied back from his face. He was somewhat fleshly at this time, though still powerfully built and possessed of a native shrewdness that made him a dangerous adversary. Now he stared down at me from the high chair; then leaned back and made a great matter of arranging his robe.

"So, you are the famous Taliesin," he said at length.

I bowed.

"We have heard many claims of your great abilities," Maelgwn said. "Are you indeed responsible for this?" He jerked a head towards the Bards.

I nodded.

"Then let us hear a song, for we are all most eager to learn how great is Elffin's Bard."

I smiled and unslung my harp from its place at my back. I took my time taking it forth from its traveling bag and tuning its strings. Then I faced Maelgwn and let the awen take me where it would.

It was then that I made what many believe to be my greatest song—though I myself doubt it. I set it down here, for what it is worth, as part of the account of these events. In it, I sang of many things that had been revealed to me in the brew of the Cauldron and afterwards as a pupil of the Wood. Much, I now see, had not then occurred; one event, at least, is still to happen. But ever, ever, I continue, and in such ways are my words made clear.

> *Primary chief poet*
> *Am I to Elffin,*
> *Though my native land*
> *Is the place of the Summer Stars.*
> *John the Divine*
> *Called me Merlin*
> *But all future kings*
> *Shall call me Taliesin.*
> *I was nine full months*
> *In the womb of Ceridwen.*
> *Before that I was Gwion,*
> *Now I am Taliesin.*
> *I was with my king*
> *In the heavens*
> *When Lucifer fell*
> *To the depths of Hell.*
> *I carried the banner*
> *Before Alexander.*
> *I know the names of the stars*
> *From North to South.*

I was patriarch
To Elijah and Enoch.
I was at the crucifixion
Of the merciful Mabon.
I was the foreman
Who constructed Nimrod's tower.
I was three times
In the prison of Arianrhod.
I was in the ark
with Noah and Alpha.
I witnessed the destruction
Of Sodom and Gomorrah.
I was in Africa
Before Rome was built.
I came here
To the remnant of Troy.[6]
I was with the Lord
In the ass's manger.
I upheld Moses
Through the waters of Jordan.
I am the instructor
Of the whole universe.
I shall be till judgment
On the face of the earth.
I have sat, in the Perilous Seat,
Above Caer Siddi.
I continue to evolve
Between the elements.
There's not a marvel in the world
I cannot reveal.

When I had done, there was silence in the hall. Maelgwn broke it at last. "A fine song, indeed," he said, and looked towards Hennin Fardd. "And what will you sing for us?"

Once again the Bard opened his mouth, but once again all that came out was the same nonsensical "blerwm, blerwm."

Maelgwn raised his brows. "I see that you have not finished," he said to me. "Is there more you would sing?"

Again the inspiration took me. I sang the song that is known as "The Reproof of the Bards" to this day, though I prefer to call it "Mocking the Mockers."

> *If you are skillful Bards*
> *of ardent awen—*
> *don't be contentious*
> *in the court of your king.*
> *Unless you know the verse forms,*
> *be silent Hennin; unless you know*
> *the name of rimiad,*[7]
> *the name of ramiad,*
> *the name of your ancestors*
> *before your own birth.*
> *And the name of the firmament,*
> *and the name of the elements,*
> *and the secret of language,*
> *and the name of your region.*
> *It's certain you know not*
> *the song upon my lips,*
> *nor the distinction*
> *between truth and falsehood.*
>
> *Why don't you flee?*

The Bard who cannot silence me
will ever be silent,
till he comes to the grave.

When I had finished, there was again a long silence. The Bards stood like sheep, staring at the floor. I had challenged Hennin Fardd and his kind on the most sensitive areas of knowledge and understanding, knowing full well they could not respond. I let the silence continue for exactly the right length of time, until I could hear the shuffling of feet and sense the restlessness of those in the hall behind my back. Then I looked at Maelgwn and demanded that he bring forth Elffin.

Maelgwn sat back in his chair and laughed. "Do you really believe I am so easily cowed?" he shouted. "I could have you flayed for this."

For answer I stood straight and let another song rise in me. It is one of which I am still proud and, in happier times, have sung again, with different results. Now I allowed all the power of the Cauldron to well up within me. I sang:

Discover what it is,
From before the Flood,
Without flesh, without bone,
Without vein, without blood,
Without head, without feet,
Neither old nor young.
Great God! How the sea whitens
When first it comes!
It is in the field,
It is in the Wood.
Without hand, without foot,
Without sign of age—
Though it be coeval
With the ages of man;

Though its years are numberless
As sand grains on the shore,
It is also as wide
As the surface of the earth;
It was not born,
Nor is it ever seen.
Its course is changeful,
Nor does it come
Whenever it's desired.
Indispensable
On land or sea,
It is without equal.
It is four sided,
It is unconfined,
It comes from four quarters
And will not be advised.
It is sonorous, it is dumb,
It is strong, it is mild,
When it travels the land,
It is silent and vocal,
It is good, it is bad,
It is there, it is here.
It is wet, it is dry,
It frequently comes
From the sun's heat
And the coldness of the moon.
It has been prepared,
Out of all creatures,
To wreak vengeance
On Maelgwn Gwynedd!

As I sang this riddle, the wind—for, of course, the answer is the wind—rose and hammered against the roof and walls of Caer Deganwy. On every side men made the sign against evil at this summoning of the very elements to my command. For a moment still I wondered if Maelgwn would give way, but after a space of time in which he stared at me with eyes in which fear and malice warred with each other, he shouted an order to two of his guards, who disappeared to return shortly with a pale and thin Elffin, still chained at wrists and ankles.

Calmly, I put my fingers to the harp strings and played a few brief chords. At once, the wind dropped, dwindling to nothing. In the silence that followed, I spoke two words in the Old Speech,[8] and the chains fell from Elffin and thudded upon the floor. I heard a gasp from a hundred different throats and had the satisfaction of seeing Maelgwn grow pale. He was no stranger to magic—though not of this kind—and I could see that he was really afraid at what I might yet do. I decided to add to the feeling. I lifted my harp and sang one further song.

> *I have liberated Elffin*
> *From the belly of the tower,*
> *Now I tell Maelgwn*
> *What his fate will be:*
> *A strange creature*
> *From the marshes of Rhianedd*
> *Will visit this place.*
> *Hair and eyes and teeth of yellow,*
> *It will bring destruction upon Maelgwn Gwynedd!*

This was enough! Maelgwn was on his feet and shouting at me to get away from his hall and himself before the last notes of my song had died away. I went to stand beside Elffin and demanded loudly whether anyone wished to prevent us both from departing. Then, when there was no movement to stop us, we walked side by side from the hall and thence from Deganwy. I had taken the precaution of bringing a spare mount and, as we rode back to Gwyddno's hall, I told Elffin all that had passed. Needless to say, he was much chastened by the experience, and never, to my knowledge, boasted about either his wife or his Bard again.

As for Maelgwn, his story does not end here, and the prophecy I had made of his death did not come about for a number of years after that. It seemed almost as though the episode of Elffin's capture drove him a little mad, for after that, he put aside Sanant and took to wife one of the daughters of Afallach, the same Gwallwenn for whom he had lusted years before. In the intervening time, she had become the wife of Maelwgn's own nephew, Cuneglassus. Now he added another murder to his list of crimes by having this lordling killed, so that he might bed with Gwallwenn.

Maelgwn's death caught up with him at last in the way I had prophesied. A terrible specter called Y Hen Wrach (The Old Hag) came to haunt the marsh lands west of Deganwy. It was said that whoever looked upon her died within hours. So fearful had Maelgwn become that he took to shutting himself up in a windowless room he had built in his fortress. But one day he heard that Y Hen Wrach had been seen near Deganwy, and his curiosity overcame his terror. He heard screams from without the room where he lay and, in great terror, he looked through the keyhole of the door.

There he saw a frightful thing. A tall gangrel, draped about with weed and rotten things, stooped low over the bodies of several guards outside. Its skin and hair and terrible eyes were all the color of ancient gold. It glanced only once in the direction of Maelgwn's hidden room, but this was enough to kill him. When his servant came later to bring him food, he found Maelgwn stretched out stark upon the floor, his flesh the color of parchment and a terrible smile upon his face.

So perished one of the great tyrants of the Island of Britain. I have seldom had, since then, occasion to exercise my powers in this fashion. Indeed, I am a little ashamed now of the dramatic way in which I chose to release Elffin. If the same thing were to happen now, I do not believe I would do it in that fashion. But I was still young, and Gwion Bach still lived in me and worked his own mischief.

Though I do not wholly understand the relationship between my master and this earlier "self" he names Gwion, it seems to me that he was never wholly free of this other, and that at times it was even painful and difficult for him to know which part of himself was responsible for the acts he performed.

AT THE WEIR

Taliesin, carried on the swift waters, sang:
"You proclaim me master of tideless currents,
Child of the daughter of unknowable love,
A light riding down to the waiting dark."
Knowledge breathed out from the Poet's lips.
The waters grew wilder before the dawn.
At last, he came to Elffin's weir,
Bearing on his brow the moon's cold light.

4
OGMA: THE SEARCH FOR THE LETTERS

 have heard it said that every race and every time must have its own savior. I know enough of the God you follow, little monk, to give him my respect. So, too, have I heard of Odin, whom the Saeson worship and who, they say, sacrificed himself to himself in order to learn knowledge and wisdom. The story I will tell you tonight is of that kind, but maybe older than any. It was told to me, ages ago, in the halls of Ceridwen at Ystrad Ffawr, as part of the knowledge possessed by the Cauldron-born who serve the Wood. It tells of the finding of the sacred letters, the Ogam—but more I will not say, for it is a mystery. Yet, for those able to see, there is a deeper lesson to learn and a key to one of the secrets of the Wood, where each kind of tree is a key to a lock that only the Cauldron-born may unlock, after long and difficult trials.[1]

I can say little of this dark story, for it seems to come from a time before enlightenment dwelled in the world. In those days, as I under-

stand it, there was no knowledge of writing in the Island of the Mighty. Therefore, the Druid kind used to commit all their lore to memory, so that in later times it was lost— some say for the best!

But writing of a kind there was, if such one may term the ancient system of markings called Ogam. These signs were used to mark boundaries and to pass messages among men. The Bards especially, such as my master, knew how to speak to each other using these symbols. Therefore, the letters were known as sacred, and it is said that the lot of humankind was much improved by their discovery. For with them, wisdom and knowledge could be set down for others to read, long after the originators of these things had turned to dust.

For myself, I prefer the letters of the Romans, though they are hard enough to write at times. Without them, these words of my master might never have been set down.

Ogma, bound on the Wheel of Taranis,[2] hung at the center of all the worlds and, as they revolved around him, dreamed . . .

Dreamed he saw again the change that came over the world he had known since it was young, saw the gods grow thin and vague as humankind forgot them, saw the face of the Mother grow dark and obscured with the smirch of a hundred fires . . .

Saw this, and much more, and knew with this seeing that he must find an answer to the need they expressed. For this he had been searching from the moment of his birth, when he stood upon the boiling rocks of the new shaped world and breathed the rich atmosphere. The thought had been there from the beginning—that he must seek for Some Thing, though what was still hidden, and that for this purpose he had been created. Dreaming still, he remembered his brothers and sisters, the Kindred of Danu[3]—bright Lugh; dark Goibhniu; mighty Bran; fearsome Macha; the terrible Morrigan; and fair Eriu, who could change herself into the most hideous Cailleach (hag). Remembered them and spoke to them again, hearing their words when he told them of his quest.

LUGH: What you are seeking is no simple thing. Take care, brother, lest you
    are lost to us . . .

MACHA: War and death walk in your train, child of Danu. Wherever you
    walk, you will be sure to meet them . . .

BRAN: The way will be hard and may take longer even than our time on earth.
    Go carefully, my brother, for I am afraid that your wounds may never
    heal . . .

Ogma listened to them all, smiled, and thanked them. Then he went forth
still in search of the Thing he had been created to find. The road was long, indeed.
It led him through ages of ages, to the thrones of kings and the battles of heroes
whose shadows grew long upon the earth. It led him to war and to despair, to love
and hatred in their many forms, but not to the Thing he sought.

Often he beheld the work of the Kindred, watched the Morrigan stride across
the field of battle with bloody hands, observed the Washer[4] with her terrible bloody
clouts, or Macha herself whirling her great arms like scythes to cut down men
who died, it seemed to him, without knowing why.

And, too, he beheld Lugh, his fiery spear striking deep into the breasts of
men, so that fire leapt within them, fire of seeking, fire of wisdom and knowledge, so that they went forth to perform great deeds, or to love, as they might, in
the face of terror and hatred and dark nightmare.

But not all that Ogma saw was dark. He himself brought light into the world.
He learned to sing the great Songs of Creation, which earned him the name Cermait,
"Honey-Mouthed," in the worlds of humankind. And sometimes he cast his own
great strength, born of the fires within the earth, into their struggles, unable to
stay unmoved when he saw good men and women needlessly oppressed.

This, too, earned him a name: Trenfher, "The Strong-Man" or "The Cham-
pion." For a time, wherever there were wrongs to set right or feats to perform,
there he went, always on foot, striding through the world, for which he was named,
sometimes, "The Walker."

And he saw the fair green face of the Mother, on whose body he walked through the ages, and he grew to love her for her changing ways, the endless patterning of her seasons, her birthing of men and women, and her receiving them back into her embrace at their life's end.

One day he met with Lugh, his brother of the Kindred, and they spoke for the first time in many ages. The god of wisdom and truth looked at the god of poetry and light and said, as he had long ago, "Beware, brother, lest you become lost to us."

And Ogma, shaking his bright head in wonder, knew how long he had walked on the earth, how far and how deeply he had sought the Thing for which he had been created. And he said, "Too long have I been absent, brother; yet I believe that I am nearing my goal." And as he uttered the thought, he knew that it was so, that soon he would find what he sought.

So the two gods parted, not without sorrow upon both sides, and Lugh vanished in a cloud of subtle light, while Ogma walked on, head up, on the dusty road.

So for a new age he walked, and humankind forgot him as they had begun to forget all of the Kindred, and the face of the earth grew dark with the smirch of fires started without reason. Almost, Ogma himself forgot who he was. Then, on a night when the stars themselves seemed almost blotted out by clouds of smoke, Ogma found rest upon a bank of dry, rank grass and slept. And in his sleeping, he dreamed . . .

Dreamed that he stood in a strange land in an unfamiliar age, beside a man who stood considering with puzzled eyes a carved picture. Ogma, too, looked at the picture and saw the figure of an old man, white haired, leading a group of others by golden chains, which stretched from his tongue to their ears. Words came unbidden to his lips, and he said, "We Celts disagree with you Greeks over making Hermes stand for eloquence. We prefer Ercwlf, who is far more powerful than Hermes. Nor should you be surprised to see him pictured as an old man, for is not eloquence often given to reaching its fullest might in old age? If old Ercwlf

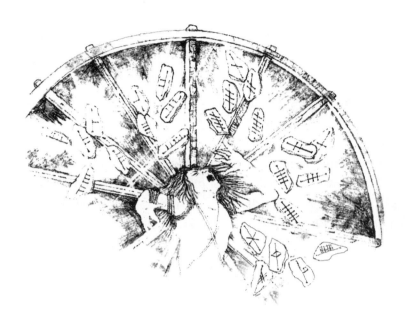

OGMA ON THE WHEEL

here drags men after him, tethered by the ears to his tongue, that should not surprise you either. You know the link between ears and tongue."[5]

With these words still echoing in his mind, Ogma awoke. He knew that the sending had been important, yet there was nothing about it that he understood, save for one thing: Ercwlf was the name by which he had been known among the peoples of the age when he had turned his strength to mighty deeds, though never had he dragged others after him by the power of his eloquence.

Rising from his rude couch, Ogma walked on, until he came to a place where he had never been before, a terrible place beyond the edge of the world, where the dead lay piled in stinking heaps, and his feet sank deep in ordure. There, on a hill of skulls, he found Taranis.

Memory stirred within him, and he remembered this last born of the Kindred, the god of fate, who could confound the careful work of his kind with a single turn of his Great Wheel. When he heard the approach of Ogma, he looked up and smiled in greeting.

"Well met, brother, are you yet upon your quest?"

"I believe, no longer," Ogma replied, knowing the words true as he spoke them. "I have come to ride your Wheel."

Taranis' eyes opened wide in disbelief. "No one in all the ages of creation has ever done so, not even a god. Why do you ask this thing now?"

"I do not know," answered Ogma, "only that I have seen that, mighty as the Kindred are, of which we are both a part, the Wheel is mightier than all, for it can change what cannot be changed and unmake what has yet to be made. Thus must I try it, for only thus will I find what I have sought so long."

"Then, brother, it shall be as you desire," said Taranis. "But even I cannot tell what might happen if you do this thing. It may even be that you will unmake everything. Knowing this, will you still attempt it?"

Ogma nodded, for the certainty grew upon him that he was come, at last, close upon the ending of his long quest . . .

Thus he dreamed, bound upon the Wheel at the hub of the turning stars, while all around him, the tides of fate swept in and out like oceans in endless flux. For as the Wheel turned, so the ages ran, winking in and out like lights in the great surrounding darkness of creation. On all sides, suns were born and died, worlds were made and unmade, civilizations rose and fell, and the children of humankind were born and lived and died in an endlessly repeated pattern.

Once, Ogma thought that he saw himself, grown young again and walking in the morning, while on every side the heavens rang with the pure notes of creation. Then the light was lost amid dark tides of hate and fear and ignorance, which swept across the face of the world like cloud shadows, without body, but gaining substance from the thoughts of humankind.

From far above, in the center of the heavens, Ogma saw that even these clouds were lit from above by the light of the sun and that it was their dark underbellies that humans saw, looking up in fear at the turning sky. And sometimes, where the winds blew strongly, the clouds were swept away, so that only

the blue of the sky showed above the world. There, men and women were happier, less fearful, and less inclined towards the ways of war and death.

From his vantage point Ogma saw, too, his own brothers and sisters of the
Kindred, going about their business in the world of humans, unaware of how he
watched them.

He saw Lugh, fiery and bright, promoting the arts of wisdom and philosophy, setting truth aflame in the hearts of humankind . . .

He saw Macha stirring men to battle in search of great glory and greater
wealth; and the Morrigan, goddess of death, taking those who fell into her dark
house on the plain of Mag Mell[6] . . .

He saw Goibhniu the Smith beating out countless swords and spears, turning then to the making of great machines of war as men grew ever more subtle in
their desire to kill and destroy . . .

He saw Bran, the Wounded One, feasting the poets and dreamers, the heroes
and the cowards, the thinkers and doers, the truth seekers and those who sank
into despair, feasting them endlessly while he told them stories that only a few
ever understood . . .

All the Kindred he saw, busy at their work. And he saw himself again, the
bright-faced wanderer who made songs that men and women could hear, so that
all might understand, at least a little, their place in the pattern of creation.

For they, too, searched for meaning, to make some sense of the fragmentary
world in which they so briefly flourished. They sought, indeed, answers to a
thousand, thousand questions through signs and symbols and glimpses of a pattern larger than themselves.

With this last thought, Ogma stirred upon the Wheel. Pain flooded his limbs,
and he felt both heavy and light at once. Turning his head with difficulty, he saw
where the rim of the Wheel curved above him, felt as well as saw the great spokes
that reached out from the center towards the edge where all was darkness, linking
them in a moving whole. And, as he looked, he saw that upon each of the spokes
was carved a sigil whose meaning he sought to understand.

Twenty-five signs he read, no two alike, though each one was linked to the others, formed in groups of five. Etched in silver they seemed, against the dark wood of the Wheel. Then he saw that each of the spokes was of a different wood: yew and oak and holly and ash and pine and birch, all set there by what art or mystery even Taranis could not have said, who but ruled the Wheel, but had not been party to its making.

Now, as his dreaming mind began to fill with images, Ogma struggled mightily against his bonds, feeling the Wheel creak and groan like a live thing, while his own bones cracked and his sinews were wrenched apart by the effort. His heartbeat thundered in his ears; pain filled every part of his body. Wracked with agony, he fought for freedom and to hold to his failing consciousness, all the while seeing the symbols of the twenty-five kinds of wood and of the trees from which they sprang.

Gradually, gathering at the corners of his mind and pouring inward upon him, darkness grew, overwhelming and drowning him as every last vestige of light was blotted out forever.

Still at last, Ogma hung upon the Wheel, which, in that moment, ceased to turn . . .

In the darkness, Ogma wandered for a long while, stumbling over broken ground, falling and rising, his dreaming mind filled with images of a dead world. Then at last he came to a place that was less dark, though he could not yet say that there was light. In this dimness, he could make out the shape of a well head, from which light dripped onto the earth. Ogma approached and looked deep into the well.[7]

A terrible blast of light smote him, all the more fierce because of the darkness he had endured. And within that light floated objects, slips of wood on which had been carved the same signs he had seen upon the Wheel. With trembling hands he drew them forth—twenty-five of them—and placed them in a leather bag he found at his belt.

For a moment, the darkness returned; then, out of it, came light. Ogma saw again, and heard, and breathed. He stood on a hill. Above him the shadow of the Wheel stretched across the earth. But beneath it lay plains of green and gold, of waving corn and soaring trees. Bright rivers threaded the land in silver stitchery. Cities of white and gold sprang up beside crystal seas; men and women walked free of shadows, no longer lost and wandering in the midnight of their souls.

As Ogma watched in wonder, the Wheel swung free, ages came and went, the patterns of creation formed and dissolved, but each made everything new. Remembering the patterns he had observed as he hung upon the Wheel, he saw now what was to be. Feeling at his waist, he found the bag with the twenty-five wooden sticks, each of a different wood, each with its own meaning, its own way of showing forth the patterns of creation.

For a moment longer, Ogma stood on the green hillside; then he set forth, down into the teeming world. Where now, at last, his search ended, he could teach the meaning of the signs of the trees to humankind, setting them free of the Wheel forever.

Thus I heard the story. I leave those who read it to make of it what they will. One thing more I shall say. I have heard tell that long after, when he had traveled the world for ages of ages, Ogma found a land where the trees had been cut down. There he planted the twenty-five staves, so that they grew to form a great forest. Many names it had, but to those who serve it now it is called . . . Broceliande.[8]

THE UNICORN

On the green hill, under the thorn tree,
the unicorn stood like a frozen wave.

Lightning played about its horn,
its hooves danced on grass.

I stood at the hill's foot,
watched the moon slide out of sight.

Through narrowed eyes I watched the beast:
archetype and symbol under a dark sky.

We each knew the other's strengths and weaknesses,
and the knowledge held us fast.

Then, for a heartbeat, poet and beast were fused,
man-unicorn, white maned and horned.

Then each was back in his own flesh,
having borrowed something of the other.

In silence I turned away.
The hill trembled to the beat of soundless hooves.

5

THE SALMON AND THE CRANE

I had many names before I became Taliesin. One of them was Finn, a name that was mine before I became Gwion and was reborn a son of the Old One. As Finn I knew much that I have since forgotten, but there are days when, as I circle the mazes of the Wood, I find fragments of old memory, which set me off upon a track of rediscovery. One such is the story I now tell, for only thus am I able to understand it.

Here my master expresses a belief that is well-known, though it is also heresy, that the soul, on its journey from the beginning of its existence to the end, periodically returns in a new body. Not many are believed to remember anything of these past lives, yet it is typical of my Lord Taliesin that he was able to recall much that would otherwise have been lost. Indeed, the stories of Finn, or mayhap Fionn,[1] are well known, but in Eriu rather than in Logres.[2] This is but another mystery among the many that surround my master's life.

I do not remember the mother whose son I was, though I believe she was the daughter of a king. My father's name was Cumhal Macart, a great warrior in the Land of Eriu. There was a prophecy that he would die in battle after he had taken a wife, for which reason he avoided women for a long time—until he met my mother, that is, and that was his undoing. For the king who was her father had also heard a prophecy, that his daughter should bear a child who would take the kingdom from him. I was to be that child, of course, though none but the Goddess herself knew that at the time.

As is the way with prophecies, my father was indeed killed in a fight over some petty thing, and my mother came to her term soon after and bore me. To forestall the prophecy, my grandfather the king ordered that I be thrown out of the window in the tower where I had my birth into the lake below the castle. And so it was done, and so might my life as Finn have ended soon enough, had it not been that my father, knowing of his impending death, had opened his heart to his own mother, who was wise in the ways of magic. And so it was that my grandmother was waiting on the shore of the lake for my first cry; and when it came, she took the wings and beak of a crane, flew up and caught me as I fell, and carried me off into the depths of the Wood—which is there in Eriu as much as here in Logres—and so to safety.

She had been prepared for my fostering, this old crane-grandmother of mine, for she had found a tree of most ancient lineage and fashioned within it a hidden chamber, so secret that not even the birds who roosted in the tree knew that we were there. And so it was that I became a son of the Wood for the first time, for the tree was a second mother to me in that life.

I *know not what my master means by this, but I believe it to be another way of talking about the mysteries of which he was initiate.*

And so I grew apace and was filled with the desire to know everything. I have heard it said that Finn—that is, myself—spent twelve years inside the tree,

MAELGWN GWYNEDD

and that when he came forth he could not even walk, so long had he remained sitting. That is not true. I lived my life in the Wood much as any other boy, save that my grandmother taught me things that others might never know in a lifetime. When the time was right, though I was still but an unfledged bird, she showed me the mysteries of the Crane.

This was the way of it.

One day grandmother woke me early. She was in human form. She did not speak, but pressed her finger to her lips and beckoned to me to follow her. We walked through the Wood for several hours, until I was tired and we came to a part of the forest I did not know. We stopped in a clearing, and grandmother bound a cloth about my eyes. Then she gave me a drink, a bitter brew that coursed like gall down my throat, taking most of my senses with it.

In the strange place where I next found myself, I saw shapes of the future forming themselves out of the mist. I believe it was then that I first saw the figure of the Ymerawdwr Arthur, though I cannot be sure, and of course, I would not have known him at that time, unless his life, indeed, extends over several incarnations. But assuredly, I saw many other things of which I shall not speak now. Then, after a time, I felt a hand gripping my arm, and I was guided through the wavering shapes of the trees.

Then the hand was guiding me no longer, and I stumbled forward unseeing, over what seemed to me a great drop, for I fell for what seemed a very long time, until I landed upon my feet. With that I entered another state of being where, though my sight was clear, I was even less certain of what was occurring. For there was suddenly another present, and She took my hand and led me, stumbling, in a dance.

Strange indeed was that dance. It seemed to me that one of my feet was suddenly lame, so that I could only hobble in a clumsy circle. Around and around I went, following She who held my hand. Around and around until my head spun anew. Yet I knew that I was approaching a center, a place where answers were to be found, and so I continued, until suddenly the hand that had held mine was gone, and a cool wind blew, and I stood alone in a clearing of the Wood surrounded by trees.

Then my old grandmother the crane-woman came towards me and kissed me on either cheek. The touch of her lips was warm, and she placed a hand upon my arm that seemed unlike her callused roughened palm. But perhaps that was part of the lingering dream; I am no longer sure.[3]

That night, and for many nights after, I dreamed. Not all of my dreams can I now recall. But one stands out above the rest. In it I wandered by a river side, and there I came upon a man fishing. He had the look of an old man, but his eyes were filled with such a merry look that I could have believed him ageless. (Indeed, he was much like Merlin, whom I knew so long after.) When he smiled at me, I asked him how his catch had gone that day, and he replied that he had caught nothing: neither then nor for many long days before. "But if you will watch with me, mayhap I shall have better luck."

So I watched, and sure enough I saw a ripple in the water, and the old man struck deep with his gaff and came up with a great, gleaming salmon, the largest I ever remember seeing. The old man was jubilant and asked me to join him and watch over the cooking of the fish while he slept. This I did, and while I watched, suddenly a blister rose on the side of the fish, and burst, and some of the hot juice fell upon my finger. I put my painful finger in my mouth, and as was to happen to me again long after when I bore another name, great knowledge and wisdom came upon me. Among the things that I knew was that the salmon was from the pool near the Well of Segais, which rises in the Otherworld, and that it had eaten of the nuts of wisdom that fell from the hazel that grows above the Well. In tasting the salmon's juices, I gained the knowledge it possessed.

Then the old man awoke, and looking upon me, he saw that I had attained what he had wished to attain, and with sorrow he said, "Long years have I sought to catch that fish, and I have grown old in the waiting. But now I see that it was meant for you. Tell me, what is your name?"

I told him that it was Finn.

Then he smiled and said, "My name is Finneces, which means 'The Old White One.' Long ago it was prophesied that one of my name should win the fish. Now I see that you were meant indeed, for you are surely 'The Young White One,' and so the prophecy is fulfilled."

I *am puzzled by my master's words here, for assuredly these names mean no such thing. I can only believe that once again he is playing a trick upon all who read these words.*[4]

Such was my dream. But I found that thereafter, whenever I had need of wisdom or knowledge, I had only to place the little finger of my left hand in my mouth, and at once whatever question I needed answering was answered for me, even though I had not known it before. Many stories are told of how I came to possess this power, such as the tale that I pursued a woman of the Sidhe, who caused my finger to be shut in the doorway to the mound from which she entered this world and departed for the Otherworld that was her home. But what I have told here is the truth, for then as now I pursue no woman, be she of Otherworldly or of mortal stock.

Thus I came by my knowledge in that life. And, when I was all but full grown, the old woman I called grandmother came to me with a bundle in her hands and gave it to me, saying that its contents had been my father's. When I opened it, I found inside a wondrous bag made of the skin of cranes. The property of this bag was that it contained the secrets of the poet's art. So then also I became a singer and made poems that are still remembered in the world. One such is this, the first that I made upon opening the bag.

May: fair-aspected,
perfect season;
blackbirds sing
where the sun glows.
The hardy cuckoo calls
a welcome to noble Summer;
ends the bitter storms
that strip the trees of the Wood.

Summer cuts the streams;
swift horse seeks water;
the heather grows tall;
fair foliage flourishes.

The hawthorn sprouts;
smooth flows the ocean—
Summer causing it to sleep;
blossom covers the world.

Bees, despite their size,
blossoms reap,
carry honey aplenty on their feet;
cattle range the mountainside.

Music of the Wood is heard,
a melody of perfect peace;
dust blows out of the house,
and mist from the lakeside.

Birds settle in flocks on the land
where a woman walks singing;
in every field is the sound
of bright water rippling.

Fierce ardor of horsemen,
hosts gathering everywhere;
on the pondside irises
are gilded by the sun.

The true man sings
gladly in the bright day,
sings loudly of May!
Fair aspected season!

Though my master does not relate the secrets of the Crane Bag, it is told that it contained the following things: the Shirt of the god Mannannan mac Lir and his Knife; the Shoulder Strap of the smith god Goibhniu, together with his Smith's Hook; also the King of Scotland's Shears; and the King of Lochlainn's Helmet; the Bones of Assail's Swine; and a Strip from the Great Whale's Back. It is also told that the bag was made from the skin of a woman who was transformed into the shape of a Crane, though what truth there may be in that ungodly thought I cannot say.[5]

Thus I became a poet for the first time, and thus I learned wisdom. After that, I returned to my father's Dun and reclaimed the lordship that had been his. And in time I grew to be the lord of many men and fought at their side as a warrior. Few there are who have not heard of Finn of the Fianna, the greatest warriors and huntsmen in all of Eriu.

But since then I have learned to set no store by such games, and so I will make no recital of them here. But of the Crane Dance I will say that it was my first meeting with She who watches and waits for me by the side of the track through the Wood. And though the Crane Bag is lost to me now, yet have I regained that wisdom that I once had, and more, through the Cauldron's brew. And here is a riddle: for as I opened the bag and took forth the wisdom of the poet, so in this life was Gwion taken from a bag as it floated in a coracle on Gwyddno's weir. And Gwyddno, Elffin's sire, had another name: Garanhir, which is to say "Crane Shanks."

THE NIGHT-HAWK

At moonrise I heard the Night-Hawk scream.
From the Hill where the Beacon flared,
I watched its fire in the green sky,
Tracing patterns above the walls of the sleeping caer.
Secret and silent I walked the old trackways,
Following their pattern through the winding dark.
Shadows closed fast around me on the wind,
And against them I sang white words.
Shards of light broke round my head.
I sang—my words were as flames that burned the air.
I waited, watching for an answer in the East,
Until a spear of light, hawk-forgotten,
Showed above the world's dark edge.
Unaware of the circling darkness, the city stirred.
I smiled at its innocent life,
Thought of its good, remembered its evil.
Weighing these thoughts I wondered
How long before I should be called again
To test my song against the Night-Hawk's screech,
Where it hung, dazed by sun, above unseeing heads.

6

THE ENTERTAINMENT
OF THE NOBLE HEAD

ecause I was one of the seven who escaped from Ireland with Bran the Blessed,[1] and because I was present at the Entertainment of the Noble Head, I must tell this story as it is given me by the awen of the Wood. And so that it may be understood by those whose task it is to understand the ways of the Wood, I will make clear those parts that are difficult, for the good of the Land. ✒ The story begins when Bran, son of Llyr, was at Harlech looking out to sea from the cliffs above Aber Henfelyn. And it begins when he said, "There is that in Ireland that I must have, for without it the Land will fail. Who will come with me to fetch this thing?" Because I was among those who said they would go, I am able to tell this story. And because I am born of the Cauldron and inhabit the mazes of the Wood, I can make it clear. ✒ Manawyddan, son of Llyr, went also, as did Nissien and Efnissien, Bran's brothers from his mother Euroswydd's side, and many others of his finest warriors to make a single shipload. I, Taliesin pen Beridd (Chief Bard), went also, because of the Land and because of the thing that

Bran sought in Ireland, which touched upon my own life.

Having left the care of the Land to his son Caradawc and to seven wise men of his choosing, Bran set sail from Aber Menai. When we were in sight of the shore, we saw men of the Land of Ireland waiting to meet us and escort us to their lord, who was named Matholwch. When we stood before him, and he asked whither we came and why, Bran made this answer, "From the Island of the Mighty we are come, seeking friendship, so that our two lands may benefit thereby."

Matholwch was well disposed to hear these words and declared that a feast should be held that very day in his own house and that Bran, son of Llyr, and all his company should be made welcome.

So all that were with Bran, including his brothers Manawyddan, Nissien and Efnissien, and myself, were seated in the house of the King of Ireland and were royally feasted. Many songs I made that night. Then when the feasting had proceeded for a time, Bran leaned his head upon one hand and said to Matholwch, "Tell me, O King, from whence had you that Cauldron in the center of the hall from which no one is ever seen to eat?"

Matholwch, drinking deep of his cup, answered, "Well may you ask, for there is a strange tale to tell concerning that Cauldron. One day when I was hunting, I came to the mound that is at the head of the lake called Lake of the Cauldron. From that vantage, I saw coming towards me a man of great size and with him a woman of strange and hideous aspect who carried that very Cauldron on her back. 'Whither are you going?' I inquired of them. And the man replied that they were seeking a place to stay, for the woman was great with child and would soon give birth.

"Now, although I misliked the look of both the man and the woman, I would not have it said that any went unhoused in my lands. Therefore I took them home with me and maintained them for a year. The woman gave birth to two children, a son and a daughter. The girl was fair, but the boy was little and black and covered in hair, so that no one wished to look upon him.

THE HEAD OF THE CAULDRON

"The pair remained in my house, but they caused such mischief with their strange ways and even stranger customs that many of the people began to murmur against them. Yet such was the power they had over me that I could not send them away and seemed almost as though enchanted by them.

"But at last I could no longer ignore the pleas of my countrymen, so I called about me my counselors and demanded that they devise a means to be rid of the terrible pair. The means they devised was this: I should have made a house with walls and roof of iron and offer it to the man and the woman. Then, once they were within and sleeping, the house should be heated with fires upon every side until all that were within should be consumed.

"This was done as had been suggested, but the outcome was not as had been foretold. Though the walls of the iron house were heated until the metal glowed white, the man and the woman were not consumed. For they dashed themselves against the walls of the house, though they were white hot, and having broken out, they fled, leaving behind the Cauldron that you see before you. Its properties are these: it will not cook the food of a coward; those who drink from it see visions; and if a man be placed into it, though he be dead, yet will he return to life and step forth whole, save only that he may not speak of what he has seen in the realm beyond."

It may be that it will be thought that the Irish King was mad to believe such things; yet these claims are not so very different from those made concerning the Cup from which Our Lord Jesu Christ was said to have drunk, which men call the Holy Grail.

Matholwch spoke with evident pride, but he could not disguise from me that he was fearful of the Cauldron and its powers. Now I rose from my place and addressed the King. "My Lord, you have not told us the names of the man and the woman who caused such great mischief in your kingdom."

"If man and woman they were," answered Matholwch. "As to their names, the man was called Tegid Voel, and the woman Ceridwen."

Evidently this Ceridwen is she that is called a goddess in certain parts of the Land. Until then I had not heard my master name her, for he always spoke of "the Old One." If the woman of the Cauldron was truly Ceridwen, then even I have heard that she is a figure of terror and might.

As though the Old One stood beside me, I heard her voice say, "I am not so easily escaped." And I knew then what I had guessed already, that the children of whom Matholwch spoke were Afagddu and Creirwy, the dark and the fair, whose lives had been so bound with my own when I was still Gwion and had no other name.[2] And so I watched as the feasting continued, and the men around me drank deeply of their cups until they fell sleeping where they sat, and silence descended upon the hall of Matholwch.

Then I saw Bran rise from his seat and begin to rouse our company. And when they were roused, Bran took the Cauldron from beside the fire and set it upon his back, and we departed, returning swiftly to our ship and setting sail at once for the Island of the Mighty.

After that, it was not long before the sails of Matholwch's fleet were sighted from the cliffs above Harlech, for angry indeed was the King of Ireland with the Son of Llyr. But Bran let not his own anger be kindled, but instead made this offer to Matholwch: he should take Branwen, his sister, as bride, so that their two kingdoms could be allied and both become more powerful. When Matholwch had consulted with his most trusted advisers, agreement was reached between the two kings, and the host of Ireland came ashore, not to war but to feast.

But at the banquet, the power of the Cauldron once again began to work upon the destiny of the Land. Efnissien, the brother of Bran and Branwen on their mother's side, came late to the feast. When he heard that Branwen was to be given in marriage to the King of Ireland, he fell into a great rage, for he said, "Branwen is the keeper of the sovereignty of the Island of the Mighty; in her blood flows the blood of Llyr and of the Sovereign Lords of the Island. Yet now, the Son of Llyr seeks to give away what rightfully belongs to all men." And so, he sought a way to prevent the marriage from taking place.[3]

*S*ome four or five leaves are missing from the writings left behind by my master, but the story can be known from the work that is known as the Second Branch of the Mabinogion. Here it is told how Efnissien mutilated the horses of Matholwch and his men, cutting off their lips, ears, and eyelids, a great insult to the laws of hospitality and to the sacredness of the horse. Bran managed to placate his guest with the gift of fresh horses and other treasures. So, the marriage of Branwen and Matholwch was celebrated, and the couple returned to Ireland. My Lord Taliesin's account takes up the story some time after this—I believe no more than a year later.

So, Branwen gave birth to a fine healthy son who was named Gwern. His parents put him to be fostered with the best of the young men of Ireland. But as time passed, there were those among Matholwch's followers, most especially his own foster brothers, who began to remember the insult done to them by Efnissien. They prevailed upon Matholwch to forbid Branwen his bed and to compel her to work in the kitchens like any common woman. Matholwch gave further instructions that the court butcher give her a box on the ear at the end of every day, which he, hands all bloody from his work, did perforce, thus adding even more to the insult already inflicted upon she who was both Queen of Ireland and sister to the ruler of the Island of the Mighty.

For the sake of her child, Branwen bore her ill-treatment in silence; but by night, she called to her one of the birds of Rhiannon who were hers to command and sent it with a message for her brother across the sea, that he should be informed of how matters stood between her and the King of Ireland.

These birds are those said to belong to the one who is named a goddess in the Books of Lore. To listen to their song was to forget the passage of time and to feel nothing but joy. I have often wondered whether Branwen's power to summon these unchancy birds shows that she was herself an initiate of the secrets of that goddess. And lest you think that here I speak of that of which I know less than nothing—and, perhaps, should not—let me say that I am as much given to curiosity as the next man, and that my master told me many things that, while I may not speak of them openly lest I be thought heretical, have caused me to form my own thoughts.

And so it was that Matholwch's swineherds, who were upon the shore of sea because the craft of swine herding might not be practiced near the dwelling of noblemen,[4] espied a great fleet of ships coming towards them from the Island of the Mighty and ran to Matholwch to tell him. He, being fearful of the might of Bran, son of Llyr, and knowing that he would have brought with him the Cauldron that he had taken from Matholwch's own land, retreated at once beyond the River Linon and broke down the bridge that was over it. The host of the Island of the Mighty drew nigh and arrayed themselves upon one side of the river, while Matholwch and the host of the realm of Ireland were upon the other.

Matholwch sent a messenger to Bran to say that he was sorry for the ill that he had done to his sister and that he was ready to renounce the kingship in favor of their son Gwern. Branwen, who had left the court of Matholwch as soon as Bran landed and hastened to join him, spoke up in favor of this offer and begged that there should be peace between the two hosts rather than that they should fight over her honor. Bran saw the wisdom of this arrangement and sent a message of friendship to Matholwch.

A great feast was prepared to celebrate the accord, and Efnissien went before the rest of the host to see that all was accomplished in a manner that would cause no slight to his brother. And so it was that he discovered a plot by certain lords among the Irish to slay Bran and his chieftains during the feast. To this end, they had placed men in leather bags that seemed as though they might hold grain or flour, and each of these they hung from one of the pillars of the hall to the number of one hundred and fifty.

This is how the story says that Efnissien dealt with them. As he passed around the hall, led by a single Irishman, Efnissien paused before each pillar and asked, "What is in this bag?"

To which the Irishman replied, "Flour" or "Grain."

Efnissien then felt about inside the bag until he encountered the head of the man within and squeezed it until the brains were crushed. This he did for the one hundred and fifty bags that hung in the hall, and when he had done, grimly he sang this englyn (an ancient Celtic verse form):

> *There is in these bags a different sort of meal,*
> *The ready combatant when the assault is made*
> *By his fellow warriors, prepared for battle.*

Whether my master truly believed this tale, I cannot say, for it is wholly fantastical. But it is said that the men of old were not like those now living, and mayhap they were possessed of such strength as to allow them to perform acts of this kind.

After this, the two hosts came into the hall from either end, and there was concord between them. The sovereignty of Ireland was conferred upon Gwern, son of Branwen, who went from one to another of the lords present to make them welcome and receive gifts from them. He went first to Manawyddan, son of Llyr, and then to Nissien, son of Euroswydd, and finally to Efnissien, who looked long at Gwern with a red light in his eyes. Then suddenly, before anyone could prevent him, he thrust the child headlong into the fire that burned in the center of the hall.

When she saw what had occurred, Branwen tried to leap after her son, but Bran restrained her, crying out in a great voice to all his men to protect his sister. In the confusion that followed, fighting began and spread quickly through the hall. The men of Ireland fought furiously, because of the treatment meted out by Efnissien to those of their number who had hung in the bags. Soon, they carried all before them and took possession of the Cauldron. And now they began to use it for the purpose for which it was intended, putting their dead warriors into it so that they came forth again living.

When Efnissien saw what was happening, he gave a great groan and said, "Alas that I should be the cause of bringing my brothers to such a strait. Evil betide me if I do not undo what I have wrought!" And so saying, he laid himself down among the Irish dead, with an Irish shield and spear in his hand, so that they put him into the Cauldron with their own dead. Then Efnissien stretched himself out and broke that which could not be broken—and burst his own heart also.

By then the fighting had gone hard with us, for though we fought with all our might, yet the Irish greatly outnumbered us, so that in the end we were cut down almost to a man. Bran himself received a wound in the thigh from a poisoned dart. Only seven escaped, together with Bran and Branwen, and made their way back to one of the ships. These seven were Pryderi; Manawyddan; Gluneu Eil Taran; Ynawc; Gorudyen, son of Muryel; Heilyn, son of Gwyn Hen; and I, Taliesin pen Beirdd. With us, we carried the fragments of the Cauldron.

When we came to land at Aber Alaw in Talebolyon, Branwen sickened and died, both for grief over her son and for the deaths of all the men of the Island of the Mighty fallen in Ireland. I made a death song for her, and we buried her in a four-sided grave on the banks of the Alaw.

Then Bran, who had spoken little since leaving Ireland, both for the pain and poison of his wound and for his sorrow over the events that had taken place, bade us travel to the Island of Gwales in Penfro. For as he said, "There all shall be made well."

When we came to that island and put to shore, we found a golden hall with high gables awaiting us, and all within prepared as for a great feast. Then Bran took the pieces of the Cauldron and laid them together so that they were joined as though they had never been broken and spoke these words: "Four score years and ten shall you remain here in joy until you open the door you see there that faces towards Aber Henfelen and towards Cornwall. In all that time, I shall be with you and a companion to each. After that time, you must cut off my head and take it to Caer Llundain (London), to the place called the White Mount, and there bury it."

There were indeed in the hall three doors, and two stood open, with the sunlight and the sounds of the sea to be seen and heard beyond them. But the third door was shut fast and barred, so that none might open it by chance.

Then as we stood in the golden hall with the remade Cauldron in the center, we began to hear a song made by three birds. And though they seemed far distant, we heard them as clearly as if they were present. And a great peace fell upon us, so that we knew them to be the Birds of Rhiannon, for it is said of those birds that those who hear them retain no memory of who they are and what has occurred to them. So it was with us, for we forgot all that had occurred in Ireland, even the deaths of Gwern and of Branwen and the wounding of our lord.

Thus we remained upon the island of Gwales for ninety years. During this time, we were feasted and entertained by Bran and knew not the passage of the years. For this was called the Entertainment of the Noble Head, which is to say, the entertainment of the noble head of Bran Pen Fair, the head of the Cauldron. Of this time I have heard tell many strange tales, such as that we cut off the head of our lord and carried it with us to Gwales in Penfro and that it contrived to converse with us. I, who was there at the Entertainment, say that this was not so. For Bran, though wounded unto death, remained, as did we all, outside of time and unable to die. Only later did we take his head, but that was after the actions of Heilyn, son of Gwyn, whose curiosity led to an ending of that time and a change in the life of the Land that only the coming of the Ymerawdwr Arthur was to restore.

Not that the people of the Island of the Mighty were aware of any of this. For the most part, they were ignorant of what had occurred, while the Land slept and the scent of honey pervaded it from the stone of gold upon which Bran, son of Llyr, lay day and night when he was not feasting or entertaining us with the wisdom that was his.

It was as though the old days were gone forever, and we dwelt in a timeless place, where the wisdom of the Otherworld was always with us. Much did I learn at that time concerning the fate of the Land, even I who had drunk of that very Cauldron that stood now in the midst of the hall upon the Island of Gwales. For Bran was wise beyond the measure of men, and indeed it is said that he was more than part god, one of the Children of Don who had come to the Island of the Mighty long since.[5]

But at last, the fourscore years and ten were passed, though we knew it not. And then it was that Heilyn, son of Gwyn, looked at the door that was shut and said, "Evil betide it if I do not open the door and look beyond it, to see if that which was said concerning it is the truth."

Then he opened the door, before any there could prevent it, and we were at once aware of the passage of time and of all that had happened to us. And Bran gave a great cry and began to sicken and die from the wound he had received. For truly is it said that those who dwell within the Otherworld may not return to their own place unless they give up all they have. And so it was that the seven who had escaped from Ireland now began to live again as mortal men, forgetting all they had known in the Entertainment of the Noble Head, as before they had forgotten the world outside. Only I remembered all that had occurred, having drunk of the Cauldron.

That vessel, indeed, we left behind us when we went forth from the island, for once Bran was dead, we did as he had instructed us. We cut off his head and took it with us to London where we buried it, with the face towards Gaul, for he had said that while it was there, no enemy would ever conquer the Land. And there it remained for many years, until the Ymerawdwr Arthur had it dug up, that it should not be said that anyone save he was Guardian of the Land. As for the Cauldron, for many years after, no word of it was heard in the lands of men. But later it played an even greater part in the story of Lord Arthur and the Wood.

*T**he greater story hinted at here was partly told to me by my master in the tale I have set down as "The Battle of the Trees," but I am sure that more of the Cauldron's history has yet to come to light.*

When we had done as we were commanded, we returned to Harlech and found that Caswallawn, son of Beli, had cast about him a veil of invisibility and had thus overthrown the seven who had been left to govern the Land. Caradawc, son of Bran, had died of grief for this betrayal.

Thus there was nothing more for the seven out of Ireland to do but return to their homes, and there live out their lives until summoned again to the Summer Lands. I alone, who still had tasks to perform, set forth again upon my wanderings, which were to lead me at length to the Ymerawdwr Arthur and his court. But that time was still many years in the future, and many things were yet to take place in the life of the Wood.

THE DOCTRINE OF INTUITION

I lie in the earth,
My birth far distant as the sun.
But my mind stretches out
To touch the shut lids of time.
I become my own god,
Bleed life into the world.
Rivers flow through my veins,
My breath assumes the power of winds.

Moon and Sun glitter from my eyes.
I offer my breast to the greedy mouth of time,
My body to the lusts of earth.
I am present at the birth of stars.
Their nature and kind I see foreshadowed,
And from their essence I am created god.
Now on my bed of earth I turn
And begin again the journey toward birth.

7
CULHWCH'S DAY

eepers of pigs and pig stealers—who can say when they are not one and the same?[1] One of the Triads[2] lists the Three Powerful Swineherds of the island of Britain as Pwyll, Lord of Dyfed; Coll, son of Collfrewy; and Drustan, son of Tallorch. Among those who are named in the same Triad as assistant swineherds are Arthur, Cai, Bedwyr, and March—surprising names to find here, but all are connected through the swine they guarded—or reaved, according to the way one chooses to see it. ❧ Many stories are told of the Sacred Pigs of the Island of the Mighty. In truth, these were the Swine of Annwn itself and brought with them both great power and great trouble. For one may not bring that which is of the Otherworld into this world without shaking the foundations of both places. Ever after, pigs have been known as strange, unworldly creatures. Not for nothing did Merlin himself, in one of his periods of madness, address his passionate words to a pig. Do you know the words, little monk? The song is a long one, but one verse runs:

Listen, little pig!
We should hide
From the huntsmen of Mordei
Lest we be discovered.
If we escape—
I'll not complain of fatigue!—
I shall predict,
From the back of the ninth wave,
The truth about the White One
Who rode Dyfed to exhaustion,
Who built a church
For those who only half-believed . . .[3]

But the time has come for me to tell one of the great pig stories—the secret, hidden, and inner story of Culhwch—for the tale that is told in the halls of kings for their amusement by Bards less adept than I tell only half, or less than half, of what might be told. For the true tale is really two stories, and it conceals truths, which are beginning to be forgotten since the Ymerawdwr went away. Also, it is a story of the Wood, which I am, therefore, bound to tell.

"Culhwch?" you may ask. "What kind of a name is that? Who would call their child 'Pig Run'?" But that strange name is part of the story, for in the name is hidden a deeper meaning than you can know, unless you are an initiate of the mysteries, in which case, you would not need to ask.

Culhwch was born without a name. Though as the son of Goleuddydd and Cilydd, he could claim descent from none other than Amlawdd Wledig himself, who was Lord of Annwn before Arawn played the game of exchange with Pwyll.[4] And Goleuddydd, being the sister of Eigr, Arthur's mother—she whom you call Igraine in the Southlands—Culhwch was also cousin to Arthur himself, which made him an important strand in the links that bound the family of the Pendragons to the life of the Wood.

When Goleuddydd was heavy with her child, she ran mad into the Wood, being unable to remain in any house until her term came. It chanced that she gave birth at last in a pig run, from which strange lying-in place, it is said, Culhwch gained his name. But that is not the whole story, as I shall show, for he had another name, which is at the heart of the tale as it is known to me, who saw all that occurred.

The true beginning of the story took place long before Culhwch was born, when Pwyll sojourned in Annwn in place of Arawn.

Here, I believe, my master refers to an old tale, still told among the Cymry (Welsh), in which Pwyll changed places with the lord of Annwn for a year, during which time Pwyll ruled in the Otherworld, while Arawn took his place as lord of Dyfed.

When Pwyll returned to the Lands Above from the Lands Below, Arawn sent him a gift: seven pigs, white as milk, save only for their ears, which were red, much like the hounds of Arawn's own unearthly pack. It is said, though I do not believe it myself, that these seven were the first pigs ever seen on the Island of the Mighty.

Be that as it may, after the death of Pwyll, the pigs were given to Pryderi, who gave them in turn to his foster-father, Pendaran Dyfed. And it was in Pendaran Dyfed's pig run that Golleuddydd gave birth to her son—"out of fear for the pigs," it is said. When Culhwch was still only a few months old, his mother died. Before she breathed her last, she made her husband Cilydd promise not to marry again until he saw a double-stemmed briar growing on her grave. In his grief, Cilydd promised, not knowing that Golleuddydd had instructed her Bard to tend the grave and see to it that no such briar ever grew there.

For years Cilydd kept his word, until, as is the way of things, the Bard forgot his task, and one day, sure enough, a briar with two heads grew upon the grave of Goleuddydd. Thus freed from his promise, Cilydd cast about for a new woman. His eye fell upon the wife of his neighbor, King Doged. As is so often the way, war ensued, with Cilydd the winner. Now we see the wisdom and foresight of Goleuddydd, for the widow of dead King Doged proved to be no good match. She sent at once for Culhwch, who had been fostered, as was the custom, with a neighboring prince, and proposed that he marry her own daughter.

Dynastically, the marriage promised to be a good one, but Culhwch had been dreaming the same dream for months past. In it, he met a girl whose look caused the sun to rise in his breast, but she never spoke to him. Culhwch was wise enough to know that somewhere, such a girl must exist, and young as he was, he set his heart upon her. His stepmother was not pleased, and so she laid a geasa (prohibition) upon him that if he would not marry her daughter, he might marry no one but Olwen, only daughter of Yspaddaden Pencawr, the most feared and fearful lord in all the seven cantrefs (regions).

That night Culhwch dreamed the dream again. This time the girl spoke to him, saying that she was indeed Olwen, the daughter of Yspaddaden. From that moment, Culhwch desired her more than life itself and vowed to set forth at once in search of his dream bride.

Now, Yspaddaden was brother to Arawn pen Annwn, Lord of the Underworld, and therefore had the blood of the Otherworld in his veins. Since Culhwch, too, had Otherworldly blood, this would have been enough to give him the right to ask for the hand of Olwen. This he would surely have done, were it not for a prophecy that held that whoever wed Yspaddaden's daughter would be the means of Yspaddaden's death. For this reason, the old chieftain had installed himself behind a ring of magical defenses and declared that no man should wed his daughter.

Knowing all of this, Culhwch decided to seek advice from someone who knew more about Yspaddaden than any man living. That man was Custennin the Herdsman, the very lord upon whom Culhwch had been fostered. Now this Custennin was a great man in his own right, but in spite of this, he had married into the family of Yspaddadan to acquire empowerment of an unworldly kind, for whoever becomes part of the great Otherworldly families gains something of their power. Yspaddadan viewed Custennin as a threat and, in a barbaric raid, killed

Custennin's two sons and many of his followers. Ever since, Custennin was possessed of a great hatred for Yspaddaden. For these reasons, Culhwch knew that if he sought to gain access to Olwen, it was to Custennin that he should go first to seek help.

Custennin listened to Culhwch in silence; then he said, "Yspaddaden must be tricked into lowering the barriers with which he has surrounded himself. If you would do this thing, you must have mighty helpers."

"Where shall I find such helpers?" Culhwch asked.

"As to that," said Custennin, "you must go to the court of our kinsman, Arthur the Mighty, for only there will you find a company that will be able to help you."

So Culhwch went his way through the Wood until he came to the court of Arthur. He demanded admittance from the porter, Glewlwyd Mighty-Grasp. Now, Glewlwyd was a man with a strange sense of humor, as well as a quick sword. When he saw Culhwch standing outside the gates in his best clothes, hair shining and newly washed, he could not resist testing him in the old way by asking him questions that only those trained as initiates should be able to answer. The exchange has since become enshrined in the tales of the Island of the Mighty, though there are few now alive who can understand it:

CULHWCH: Is there a porter at the gate?
GLEWLWYD: There is. And you, with the wagging tongue, what do you ask
    of me?
CULHWCH: To open the gate.
GLEWLWYD: I will not.
CULHWCH: Why not?
GLEWLWYD: The knife is in the food, the drink is in the cup, and a great
    throng is in Arthur's court. Except you are a king's son, or a musician
    who brings his art, or a craftsman his craft, you shall not have entry.
CULHWCH: I have been in Caer Se and Asse, in Sach and Salach, in Lotor

and Fotor. I have been in Caer Rigor and Caer Fandwy, in Caer Ochren and Caer Goludd, in Caer Siddi and in Caer Feddwit. And if the door is not opened to me, I will raise three cries of distress outside these gates that shall be heard in every part of the Land and shall cause women with child to miscarry. Therefore, open to me who is cousin to Arthur the Mighty and would claim the right of speech with him.

Thus Culhwch revealed that he knew the secret names of the Otherworld (though indeed there are many more that he did not reveal) and showed that he knew also the speech of the initiates. Thus he gained entry and was taken to Arthur.

The first request Culhwch made was an ancient one. Not a man had asked it of the Ymerawdwr in living memory. That request was that Arthur trim Culhwch's hair. By this strange request, he established the blood tie between them and made it impossible for Arthur to refuse his further requests, even had he wished to do so.[5]

So the High King took up his golden shears and trimmed the youth's hair. Then he asked what further boon he might grant his young cousin. Culhwch explained that he wished to marry Yspaddaden's daughter and requested of the Ymerawdwr that he send men of his warband to aid him in his suit.

To this request Arthur also acceded, even to leading a party of warriors to Yspaddaden's gates to ask the hand of Olwen for his cousin Culhwch. Nine gates protected Yspaddaden from the world of men, every one guarded by unseen sentinels. At Arthur's request, each gate opened silently before them, so that they could enter. But when at last they stood before Yspaddaden, there was scarcely a man there who did not quail, for he was grim indeed. Of more than mortal height and dressed in a great bearskin robe, he wore upon his head an ancient helm that had as its crest a snarling boar. Across his knees lay a black and ancient sword, notched from many battles, which he stroked as he listened while Arthur spoke in Culhwch's name.

At length, Yspaddaden laughed, though there was no mirth in the sound, and said, "None may seek my daughter unless he first achieve a task that I shall set for him."

"What task is that?" demanded Arthur.

"As to that," answered Yspaddaden, "he must obtain the comb and sheers from behind the crest of Ysgithrwyn, the Chief Boar, so that I may be shaved with them in preparation for the wedding."

Arthur stood up very straight and said, "It shall be as Yspaddaden Pencawr requests. Our cousin shall obtain these things, and in return, he shall have the marrying of Olwen." With that, the company quit the dark hall, with the sound of Yspaddaden's laughter ringing in their ears.

Now, you must know that this was no ordinary task that had been set for Culhwch. For this Ysgithrwyn was no ordinary beast. He was, indeed, after the mighty Trwch Trwyth, the greatest prize in all the Island of the Mighty. Indeed, there are those who say that the Great Hog Hunt came about because of Culhwch's request, but that hunt was of another kind, while this was for a lesser beast and in a different cause.

My master here makes a distinction between two of the great boar-like creatures that were hunted by the Ymerawdwr and his men. In the first instance, the quarry was the mighty Trwch Trwyth, who seemed in some way—I am not certain how—connected to the secret heart of the Land. In the second place, the hunt was for the beast known as the Chief Boar, the history of whose chase is here recorded. A third hunt for the great white sow Hen Wen brought great destruction to the Land, as I have set down in the story called "The Hunting of Hen Wen."[6]

Now in all this time Culhwch had not caught so much as a sight of Olwen, and in his heart he longed to speak with her. It so happened that, as the company left the Caer of Yspaddaden, they passed close by a place where there was a pig run, and the thought came to Culhwch that he might thus get a message to Olwen. He begged leave of Arthur to turn aside from the road.

Now the swineherd's name was Coll, son of Collfrewy, who was, as I have mentioned, one of the Three Powerful Swineherds of the island of Britain. The swine that he guarded were descendants of the seven swine that had come out of Annwn. The greatest of them was named Hen Wen, that is, "Old White One." A prophecy concerning this beast held that one day she would cause great sorrow to the men of Britain. Later, Arthur would hunt her and all her litter, with intent to kill them all, but that time was still far off. Culhwch asked Coll if he would take a message from him to Olwen.

"I will do it," Coll said, "if you and your company will remain here and keep watch over my swine."

To this Arthur agreed, and thus it was that the Ymerawdwr, together with Cei, Bedwyr, and Drustan, son of Tallorc, became swineherds that day and watched over the very pigs that they would one day pursue, and they are thus remembered in the Triads.

And so the company waited. Presently Coll returned. With him came Olwen herself—white-armed Olwen of whom it was said that where she walked, white trefoils sprang up behind her, so that she was called Olwen White Footprint. There was not a man there but felt the tide of passion rise in him at the sight of her. But she had eyes for no one save Culhwch, and the two went apart and spoke together.

"I would win you, lady," said Culhwch.

"Then you must first kill my father."

"I do not know how to do that."

"Only one weapon is strong enough to take his life and that is the Sword of Light that is held by his kinsman Wrnach. If you have the strength and the courage to take it, and if you can achieve the test that has been set you, then you will succeed."

"That shall I try," said Culhwch. Olwen then gave him directions how to find the court of Wrnach, though she warned him that it would be far from easy to win the sword.

Culhwch told Arthur what Olwen had said, and though this additional quest was more than he had promised at first, the Ymerawdwr agreed to accompany his nephew to the court of Wrnach. When they arrived, Culhwch declared that winning the sword was a task that he must perform alone to prove himself worthy of Olwen. And he went and knocked on the door.

The porter came and said that none might enter unless he brought some craft with him.

"I have a craft," Culhwch said.

"What is it?" the porter asked.

"I am a wright."

"We need one not," the porter replied.

Culhwch said, "Wait. Question me further. I am a smith."

"We need one not. Go hence from here," the porter said angrily.

"Wait, question me further. I am also a harper."

"And I say again, we need one not. Now go, before I call the warriors of the house."

"But," said Culhwch, "I am a leech also. Have you no need of such a one?"

"We have one already," said the porter, getting ever more enraged.

"Then let me say one word more. I am the finest burnisher of swords in the whole of the Island of the Mighty."

This time the porter hesitated. "We have no such man. I will ask my lord." And he went forthwith to Wrnach and told him what Culhwch had said.

Wrnach declared that he had been seeking someone to clean the blade of his sword these long months past, and he bade the porter to admit the youth.

So Culhwch came into the hall where Wrnach sat. The old lord, one-eyed and scarred from many battles, sent for his sword. When it was brought, Culhwch drew forth a whetstone and began at once to work on the blade. As he worked, he sang beneath his breath an ancient spell of wakening that he had learned from Olwen:

Blade of light,
Sword of might,
Waken now,
Defend the right.

Blade of Sun,
Sword of Truth,
Foes of light
Destroy each one.

As Culhwch worked, the sword sang back to him, wordlessly. Soon the blade was as bright as the sun itself and sparkled in Culhwch's hand like a flame. Then, before anyone could prevent him, Culhwch rose up and struck down Wrnach. Then he fought his way through the press of the old lord's men until he won through to the outer court and so away. For this deed, he afterwards received a new name, Goreu, which means "the best."

After this, the company returned to the High King's place, and Arthur sent forth men to seek out the lair of the Chief Boar Ysgithrwyn. It was not long before word came of the beast, and a hunting party set off at once in pursuit of it. In that party were Cai, who could go for nine nights and nine days without sleep; and Bedwyr, who could travel more swiftly than any man in the whole of the Island of the Mighty; and Gwrhyr Gwalstawd Ieithoedd, who spoke the language of bird and beast; and Gwalchmai, son of Gwyar, who never returned home without what he went forth to seek. Also there were Trachmyr, who was Arthur's chief huntsman; and Gweir Gwynn of the Long Spear; and Llwydeu, son of Cilcoed, who could hear an ant crawling more than ten leagues distant; and Gilla of the Stag's Leap, who could cross a hundred leagues in one bound. All these, and many more, to the number of half the teulu (the hundred warriors of Arthur's court) went in search of the Chief Boar. Leading them was Arthur's own hound Caval, and the two bitches of Rhymi, Gwyddrud and Gwyddneu, with all the pack of the Ymerawdwr of the Island of the Mighty.

YSGITHRWYN

Before three days had passed, they raised Ysgithrwyn from his lair. Then they went, in full cry, after the Great Boar, for the space of two days and two nights. And in all that time, they ceased not from riding, nor rested, nor slept. At the end of it, they caught Ysgithrwyn, who turned at bay, rent many of the hounds, and pierced the bodies of three of Arthur's men.

Then, seeing how things fared, and noting where the comb and shears gleamed behind the crest of the great beast, Culhwch rode alongside and threw himself upon its back. There he hung, and there stayed, while he drew forth the comb and sheers from the thick bristles of the boar's crest. Then he threw himself off Ysgithrwyn's back, and the great beast fled furiously away, too fast even for fleet-footed Bedwyr to catch him, and so was lost for that time to the hunt.

But Culhwch was well pleased with his spoils and set off at once for the court of Yspaddaden Pencawr, with the heroes of Arthur at his back, all steaming and sweating from the hunt. As they drew near the first of the nine gates that stood between the hall of Yspaddaden and the world beyond, Culhwch held aloft the bright shears and the great comb and cried aloud that he had achieved the task set for him. "Therefore," he called out in the same ringing voice, "keep now your promise, great Yspaddaden, or be known for all time as a false lord."

At these words, the doors flew open on silent hinges, though none could see who it was that worked them, and the hunting party came again before the doors of Yspaddaden's hall. Culhwch flung them wide and marched inside. There sat the lord of the place, as huge and old and terrible as before, with his great jutting brows and ragged beard, glaring evilly from his bloodshot eyes. As Culhwch and his band looked at him, it seemed for a moment that they saw another shape there, a great bristled boar shape that grinned and gnashed at them in rage.

"See!" cried Culhwch, holding up the comb and shears, "I have come to be my lord's barber!" And he took the comb and the shears and shaved Yspaddaden. And it is said that this was a most cruel shaving, for it took not only the hair from his head and the beard from his chin, but also his ears and the flesh of his crown. Then, when he had done that, Culhwch dragged the old man from his chair and cut off his head with the great sword that had been Wrnach's, so that Yspaddaden lay dead in his own hall.

Then all the company of Arthur hailed Culhwch a hero, and Olwen came to stand by his side, as was her right. And from that moment the lovers were parted no more in that life, but were content with each other and ruled over the lands of Yspaddaden wisely and well. It is said that they invited Custennin to join them, which he was glad to do, for thus was an old score settled.

Thus it was, as I, Taliesin, Primary Chief Bard of the Island of the Mighty, tell it; and thus have you seen the stages by which young Culhwch made his way from nameless boy to husband of Olwen, daughter of the Otherworldly kingdom, who is the prize in this story, just as Sovereignty was the prize for young Geraint,[7] or the Cup of Immortality for Galaad.[8] And if you are able to recognize the steps by which Culhwch reached his goal, then you possess a secret that is not revealed to any who are not initiates. I speak of these things now only because we live in a time that is in danger of forgetting them.

*W*hat did my master mean by this? I have puzzled over this story for many long days, and still it remains the most mysterious of all the tales he told me.

I remember only one thing more that he said of it: that it was a matter of question and answer, of exchange and empowerment. I believe that he meant to say that the old lord, Yspaddaden, was at the end of his term in the Otherworld. For it is clear to me that much of what the Lord Taliesin described here could not have taken place, if at all, in this world. Culhwch, he of the strange name, was the Challenger who, with the help of the Lord Arthur, deposed the old lord and became his substitute.

Of one thing at least I am certain, though I can offer no explanation for it: in some way, Yspaddaden and the Chief Boar were one and the same, though how this could be I know not. And I believe that I see certain patterns in the questions that were asked at the Court of Arthur and the Court of Wrnach. But beyond this I may not go; others may read these words who know better than I, though I doubt if they will fully comprehend the wisdom of the Lord Taliesin, who told me these things.

THE RECONCILIATION OF OPPOSITES

I am the reconciler.
I hold the opposites in either hand
And, without letting them approach,
Allow them to commingle.
In the moment of reconciliation
I am the center,
The tree at the storm's heart,
The reflection of true night,
An alembic of light and dark.

As the waves of silence rise,
The land shudders—
But the blow never falls.
Held back by their measured strokes,
All time teeters,
Falls from my steady hand
Like grains of winnowed wheat.

My words themselves
Are a balance and a blending
Of wisdom and folly.
I have seen to the heart
Of the rosy Grail;
Where the Cauldron gleams
I have drunk.

Madness is not my measure.
Love is now my tomb.

8

ISKANDER AND THE SHOW-STONE

n the Wood it is possible to travel without ever moving. You may see the Wood, if you wish, little monk, as a kind of map, existing in more than one dimension. Thus, to move horizontally from one clearing to another may be also to move vertically in time and space. Once I learned this, I was able to be present at many events that were part of the work of the Wood. Thus I watched over the birth of Arthur, even though I knew nothing of his life until long after, and in the same way, I was able to watch over the search for the Cauldron and the Grail as though they were separate, rather than parallel, events. ✥ It was thus that I encountered Iskander (you would know him better as Alexander, little monk). It was on a day when I wandered in the thousand-branching ways of the Wood. I was not seeking anything. My mind lay idle, and the Wood was silent. Then, before me, there opened up one of the clearings I had learned led to other places and sometimes to other times. Not that they who enter there move through time, but such places exist in more than one dimension at the same moment. As I entered, I felt a familiar shudder in my flesh, a ripple in the air. Then I stood no longer in the Wood—though I retained an awareness of it still— but in the sandy inlet of a river. The sun beat down from a brazen sky, and the heat of the place told me that I was no longer in the far West but had moved into another place.

The river ran sluggishly, much of it mud with only a thin trickle of water towards the center. As I looked at it, I became aware of a man sitting on a large flat rock, which jutted out over the river. I was amused to see that he appeared to be fishing. Then I heard him muttering, in a language I recognized as Greek, "It must be here. Gods! Help me! I must find it!"

I looked into the muddy water and with the gift of Sight saw where something glinted on the bottom, a few paces downstream from where the man had hung his line. "You will find what you seek down there," I said, indicating as near as I could where the object lay.

The man hardly started at all. He looked up at me with a pair of extraordinarily bright blue eyes, set in one of the most handsome faces I had ever seen. After a moment he looked again at the river, following the line of my finger. Then he shrugged, threw down the line and, with the lithe grace of an athlete, jumped down into the ooze and waded through it to the point I had shown. "Here?" he asked.

"Another pace—there!" I replied.

He thrust his hand into the water and came up holding the thing I had seen. He gave an exclamation of satisfaction.

"My thanks to you, whoever you are."

"I am Taliesin," I said.

"Iskander."

I knew at once who he was. The Conqueror. The one whose name is still called in the same breath "the Great One." He who had once ruled half the world, whose military genius had made him feared by all who opposed him. Death had claimed him young, I recalled—poison, probably administered by the hand of a jealous follower.[1]

I turned my attention to the object in his hands. It was a small stone, oval in shape, fitting Iskander's palm comfortably. I saw that it was an object of great power, probably one of the Show-Stones of which there were perhaps five in all the world. I had not known that Iskander possessed such a one, though it explained a little his uncanny genius for knowing the thoughts of his enemies. He saw my eyes rest on the Stone and held it out before him, almost, I thought, eagerly.

"Do you know what this is?"

"I believe it is a Show-Stone."

"Then you are not of this world. Yet you do not look like a god. What, then, are you?"

"Nothing more than a traveler," I said, "one who makes songs for great lords such as yourself."

"Then you have heard of me?"

"Who in all the world has not?"

"And what do they say? That I am a power-hungry tyrant, seeking ever to expand my realm?"

"I have heard that you are the greatest soldier of your day, and that you are a scholar who pursues truth through all the world."

He was silent for a moment. Then, "You speak as though I lived in the past. Are you, then, from the future?"

I nodded my assent.

"With this," he held up the Stone, "I am able to see many things, but never what is to be, except in a shadowy way sometimes. Do you know my future?"

"Some little part," I said, "but if you know aught of the ordering of the world, you must know also that I am forbidden to speak of such things."

"Then you are an initiate."

I recalled that I had heard how Iskander kept an open mind toward all beliefs and that he himself was initiate of many mysteries. I answered with a sign that all who have walked the chosen path may recognize. Iskander answered in kind.

"Come," he said. "My tent is but a league from here. Join me, and let us converse."

Thus it was that I came to be sitting in the tent of the great Iskander, sipping a cool drink the taste of which I can still recall with pleasure, while we spoke of many things. Mostly, I listened to him, for while I might say nothing of his future, he could and did tell me much of his own life, of the struggles he had endured after the death of his father, Philip of Macedon, before he won recognition and began the extraordinary career that was to make many believe him a god.

"You may wonder, my friend," he said, sipping carefully at his fifth cup of wine—he was not drunk, but I sensed a loosening of the iron control in which he habitually held himself. "You may wonder what it is that drives me to seek still further conquests. I will tell you. It is this . . ." He touched the Show-Stone that hung now in a plain leather bag around his neck. "It seems there is always a price to pay for possessing such things. Yes, it has enabled me to conquer my foes with ease, but it has given me a hunger, a curse for which there seems no cure, a thirst for knowledge I cannot slake. Do you understand this?"

I nodded. "Such things are not unknown. I have seen other men driven by such desires." I thought of Merlin as I spoke, locked in his tower of glass, endlessly searching the stars for meaning.

I found Iskander's penetrating gaze bent upon me. If I had thought him relaxed for even a moment, I saw now that he was not, that he was about to ask me a question he had been formulating from the moment he learned who—or what—I was.

"I want you to help me to be rid of this thing." He touched the bag containing the Stone again. "Take it back with you, Taliesin, into your own place and time."

For a moment, I hesitated. What he wished was just barely possible by the laws of the Wood, but I knew, at the same moment, that I could not do what he wanted. To take the Stone would be to bring something into the Land of Britain that was not meant to be there. I knew this as surely as if I heard the voice of

Merlin or the Lady telling me. Just as I heard, too, the note of concealed desperation in the voice of the Lord of the World.

"Why did you not simply leave it where it was just now, in the river?"

"For some other to find and perhaps use against me? Nay, that might I never
do." I knew, as he spoke, that this was only half the reason. Such things were
more than hard to rid oneself of.

"What you ask I may not do," I answered at last, "but there may yet be a way
for you to be rid of the Stone, if that is what you truly desire."

"It is my dearest wish," Iskander replied with no change in his voice to
betray the depth of his feelings.

"First, I must know how you came by the Stone."

"That is soon told. I had it from an old beggar who stood upon the road of
my army as it marched towards the East. When my guards would have pushed
him aside, he called out to me, naming me "Lord of the World," which none had
called me until then. In curiosity, I stopped and spoke with him. He told me that
a great future awaited me and that the Stone would bring me luck. From the
moment I took it, everything changed. I could see all that I needed as if in a glass.
Since then, all power has become mine, and I have never failed in any course I
have taken. Yet still, I would be rid of it. For who can own such a thing and
continue to believe in his own worth? Perhaps I would have done everything I
have done without the Stone. Perhaps not. With it, I am great, but troubled. If
there is anything you can do to help me be rid of it, you will have served me
well."

While he spoke I had been thinking. Now I said, "Let me hold the Stone for
a moment."

Iskander did not hesitate. He opened the little leather bag and, taking forth
the Show-Stone, put it into my hand. It lay there, for all the world like a plain bit
of rock, but I felt its power and knew its source. Even for that moment I felt a
desire to keep it, to take it back to Britain in Arthur's day, to use it, as I knew I
could, to help preserve the dream of Logres. But after a moment, that feeling

passed. I half tasted the bitter drink of the Cauldron on my tongue as I gave it back to Iskander.

"Will you promise to do all that I tell you, without question?" I demanded.

And indeed, little monk, the Lord of the World, at whose signal kingdoms could be wiped from the memory of the world forever, nodded his head. "Whatever you ask of me, I shall do it, without question."

"Then come." I rose and left the silken tent. Iskander followed, bidding his guards remain at a discrete distance. We walked back to the river bank, and I sought the return way into the Wood. But, instead of entering again the clearing amid the trees from which I had come, I used the moment in which we stood between the worlds to turn aside, willing myself, and Iskander with me, into another place.

We emerged at the edge of a sea. I heard Iskander draw in his breath, but I had no time to explain what I was about. Instead I took his arm and hastened into the water. He scarcely flinched as the waves closed over our heads and we continued walking, downward, as if we were upon an ordinary road. Because part of ourselves existed elsewhere—myself in the Wood of Broceliande; Iskander by the Eastern river bank—we had no difficulty breathing and, in a short time, came to the place I sought.

A great cavern opened before us on the bed of the sea, and we went within. Intricate scrolls of coral decorated the walls of the place, and strange creatures, half-man, half-fish, watched us from the shadows with huge eyes. But I kept my face firmly to the fore and walked directly into the cavern, Iskander at my side, until we stood before a coral throne on which sat a huge figure with scales for skin and a wild entanglement of hair like seaweed half-obscuring his face. Horns grew from his brow, and his eyes were as cold and fathomless as the sea itself.

I bowed low before the King of the Waters and indicated Iskander. "Here is a Lord of the World who comes to offer you a gift. Will you take it?"

A low rumble filled the cavern. It was the Sea King's voice. I heard him say: "I have no need of such things. Perhaps my brother in the Heavens will take it."

He was neither well, nor ill, disposed. Like so many immortals, by whom the existence of men was tolerated, the Sea Lord neither cared for nor took thought of the world above, save where it touched his power. Without more ado, we were dismissed by a wave of a great webbed hand and found ourselves shooting up through the water like bits of flotsam caught in the tide. The strain of keeping Iskander at my side, while his soul longed to return to its body, was beginning to tell, but with redoubled effort I reestablished a sense of equilibrium.

We shot forth from the water and fell upwards through the sky towards the arch of the heavens. Like twin arrows, we etched a track across the sky and entered a place where the winds met and buffeted one another and then were still. Clouds surrounded us, with presences within them we could only half see, though we knew them to be there. At the heart of this strange, shifting landscape, we came upon a figure whose outlines were as blurred as his realm, yet his eyes, when he looked upon us, were as clear as those of his brother in the sea, and his voice, when he spoke, had all the songs of the wind within it.

"Why do you come, little men?" he boomed, and for answer I touched the bag that hung still round Iskander's neck, for he was bereft of words in his wonder at this journey.

The Lord of the Winds stretched forth a great hand, and after a moment of hesitation, Iskander drew out the Stone and placed it in the center of the huge palm. Great fingers closed around it briefly, and when the hand opened, the Stone had become so much dust, which blew away in the winds that played about that place.

Followed by the booming laughter of the Lord of Air, we fell again, swiftly but always safely, back down the sky. Feeling more tired than I had in many years, I directed my thoughts towards the place where I had first met Iskander. In another moment we had landed, and the Lord of the World turned to give me breathless thanks.

"I know not what the future holds for me," he said, "nor do I wish to know. But I am glad indeed to be rid of the Stone, which has been more curse than blessing." He hesitated. "If there is any reward I can offer a traveler such as your-self, you have only to name it."

There was nothing I wanted save to return to my own time and place. Still, I believe that all labors are worthy of reward, and I had a fancy to take back something that would remind me of my meeting with Iskander. My eye fell upon a magnificent gold ring on his finger. It had the shape of a lion upon it, and I remembered that to some he was known as the Lion of Macedon. So I asked that if it were not an especially precious thing, I would like it, for memory's sake.

Iskander took off the ring and gave it to me with a smile. "I do not know if I have been dreaming, or whether I still dream," he said, "but I thank you for taking me on such a journey."

I took the ring and stepped sideways into the return way to the Wood. It is said that the fortune of Iskander changed from that day, and that soon after, he was poisoned by his servant who was in the pay of an enemy. I fancy that he died happier knowing himself rid of the Show-Stone. I kept the ring and still wear it on occasion, in token of that meeting. After, I made this song for him:

> *Why does the sky not fall*
> *Now the Lord of the World is dead?*
> *Iskander the Great,*
> *Iskander of Macedon,*
> *Hurling his thirsty spears.*
> *Mighty in his weapon-lore . . .*
> *He went to the sea bed,*
> *In pursuit of fate;*
> *He went upon the wind*
> *To seek good fortune.*
> *He saw the world*
> *In all its grandeur.*
> *That which he desired*

He won; that which he lost
Was lost forever.
In death he won
Rest for his spirit.[2]

THE SONG OF THE WIND

Taliesin heard the roaring of the wind.
He listened to its dark iron voice.
From the trees' shelter he walked with it
As it led him by hill and stream,
Leant him wings to leap the land.

Beyond the dark hills, by trembling walls,
Walking with the wind's wisdom,
Taliesin sang through Logres,
Sang the wild songs of death and renewal,
Went out upon the shores and called the waves,
Gave back song for song from the Singing Head,
And in the wind knew matchless wisdom for his own.

9
THE BATTLE OF THE TREES

ecause of the Wood, whose thousand-branching ways are mine to travel as I will through the power of the Old One and the drink of awen, I am the master of trees and of growing things. Thus when it came to finding how I might serve the Land in the battle between the Children of Don and the Lord of Annwn, I was enabled to bring the very forces of the Land itself to fight. In this way I was able to observe still further the unfolding of the story of the Cauldron, the Wood, and the Sleeping Lord.[1]

My Lord Taliesin spoke often of these three mysteries in all his works. The Cauldron is that vessel from which he was himself renewed, as has been told; the Wood is that region that he refers to again and again as Broceliande. In it many strange and terrible beings had their home. The Sleeping Lord is, I believe, that same Bran the Blessed of whom we have heard tell, and also, perhaps, the Ymerawdwr Arthur, whose history is fully told in my master's own great Chronicle.

So let us hear of Amatheon, son of Don, who was lord over the cantref of Dyfed, and his brother, Gwydion, son of Don, who was lord over the cantref of Gwynedd.

Now, despite the friendship that had been between Arawn, lord of Annwn, and Pwyll, who had been lord of Dyfed in the time before Amatheon,[2] this good feeling had lapsed. The chief cause of this quarrel was the way that Arawn liked to hunt over lands adjacent to his that were above ground—the greater part of his realm being below the earth, in the Hidden Realm where no man went. Night after night, the white-bodied, red-eared hounds of Annwn could be seen and heard in Gwynedd or Dyfed in pursuit of quarry, and though Gwydion and Amatheon repeatedly sent word to Arawn forbidding him to hunt their lands, he did not listen but continued in his ways.

So it came about that on a certain day, when Amatheon was at his chief seat at Harlech, Gwydion came before him and said: "Brother, last night the red-eared hounds of Annwn hunted again on my lands. In recompense, I propose that we two go into the realm of Annwn and capture the White Roebuck and the Hound of Gwythyr, Arawn's greatest prizes except for the Cauldron that Bran brought out of Ireland, which no man may look upon unscathed."

Amatheon agreed. That very night the brothers left Harlech in secret and rode to the borders of Annwn. There, Gwydion used his magic to cast a cloak of invisibility around them both, while they waited at the mouth of Uffern, the cave of darkness that led into the realm of Annwn. After a while, they first heard and then saw Arawn himself upon his white steed, leading his pack of white-bodied, red-eared hounds to hunt once more in the lands of men.

When the way lay silent at last, Amatheon and Gwydion stole quietly into the mouth of Uffern and followed the winding way deep into the earth. Gwydion went before and used his magic to light the way, until they came at last into the heart of the underworld kingdom, by whose pale, gray light they were able to see how best to proceed.

Gwydion, who was wise and skilled in magic beyond any man then living in the Island of the Mighty, knew well where they should look to find the White

Roebuck and the Hound of Gwythyr, for they were kept together within a fence of plaited branches outside the dark palace of Arawn. And from this same enclosure had once come the magic pigs given as a gift by Arawn to Pwyll, lord of Dyfed. But they found that to get into the palisade was no easy task, for it had upon it a lock that no man might open unless he knew the key. But Gwydion laughed and sang this englyn:

> *Perfect my art in the land of Annwn.*
> *No lock or door refuses me*
> *Because of the power of the name.*
> *Achren art thou called, of Arawn's making;*
> *Open, therefore, to the son of Don.*

The lock burst open with a great noise, and Amatheon and Gwydion entered. They put upon the White Roebuck and the Hound halters that Gwydion had prepared in readiness, and thereby took them out of the enclosure and returned by the way they had come to the lands of men.

"Now may we see an end to the hunting of our lands by the Lord of Annwn," said Gwydion. But that day there came a messenger from Arawn, who demanded the return of the Roebuck and the Hound, which were his greatest prizes except for the Cauldron of Bran.

Amatheon returned this answer: "Many times have I and my brother asked that the Lord of Annwn cease to hunt upon our lands, and many times has he refused us. Now we have taken that which is his in recompense."

When Arawn heard these words, his anger knew no bounds. At once he began mustering his armies to attack Amatheon and his brother. Terrible indeed were his forces, for all that is most fearful to men is to be found in the lands beneath the earth, and hard it was to slay any of them, both because of the power of their Lord and because of the Cauldron, which gave back life to the dead.[3]

So it was that when word of the mustering of the hosts of Annwn came to Amatheon and Gwydion, they began to think how they might defeat their enemy.

THE UNNAMED ONE

Now must I tell something of the history of the Cauldron after the death of Bran and the sundering of the Company of the Noble Head. For at that time, as I have told elsewhere, the Cauldron had remained behind upon the island of Gwales, and there it stayed until Arawn heard of its whereabouts and went himself to the golden hall to fetch it. Now it lay in the heart of his dark castle in Annwn, from which no man then living could bring it forth. Such was the power of the Lord of Annwn.

Yet not all were powerless against the Cauldron's working. Much had I learned of its nature and history since I had journeyed with Bran to Ireland. Having heard of the quarrel between Gwydion and Amatheon and the Lord of Annwn, I traveled to be with the brothers in Harlech to offer them aid. My journey was urgent as I knew of another reason, which the awen told me, that would make it hard for the brothers to be victorious. Therefore I spoke up. "Hard will it be to defeat this host. Yet I will chant a song that will prevent the working of the Cauldron for a time. If you can find a way to slay your enemies, you may know them truly dead. But there is one among the men of Annwn that you cannot defeat unless you have his name. And that name is hidden from all men."

But Gwydion smiled and said, "We also have among our number one whose name is hidden, and unless it be known, our host may not be defeated."

Thus it was that the armies of Amatheon and Gwydion, sons of Don, and the army of Arawn pen Annwn, Lord of the Underworld, met in battle at a place named Goddeu Brig. And I, as I had promised, stood upon a hill that overlooked the field of conflict and made a song that caused the Cauldron to fail, so that when Arawn's lieutenants put a slain warrior into it, he remained truly dead, and the advantage that Arawn had thus was lost.

mhen I questioned my master about the nature of this song and what it might contain, he looked at me with cold fire in his eyes and said that if he were to sing it, the consequences would be much worse than I could contemplate. I asked no further questions of this kind and trust that those who read these words may know better than I what was meant.

All that day the two hosts struggled mightily against one another, and many men fell upon both sides. But neither might prevail against the other because of the warrior within each host whose name was hidden. And all day Gwydion sought by means of his magic to discover the name. But he could not, and when the battle ceased that night, more than a thousand men lay dead upon the field, and the ravens feasted well upon them.

Gwydion thought deeply and set to work to provide a new army for the next day. The way that he did it was thus: He sent out men to gather branches of certain trees whose very names and powers were sacred to the Island of the Mighty and to the Wood. (Many, indeed, were the same as Ogma of old had gathered from the Wheel of Taranis.) Then he and I together devised a song that would bring them to life for a day. In the ranks of the host each man was given a sprig of one of the sacred trees, such that he who held the Oak was captain over the warriors of Oak; and he that held the Rowan was captain over those trees, unto the number of one hundred trees that were represented in the battle. It is said that certain trees were not present because they grew not in that part of the Island of the Mighty. But many there were that grew there, so many that the next day, when the hosts of Gwynedd and Dyfed were arrayed against those of Annwn, they were mighty indeed. Nor might the army of the trees be easily overcome, for though they had upon them the likeness of men, yet were they tough and grim, and few were the weapons that made more than shallow cuts upon them.

Then it was that I first sang the song that is known as "Cad Goddeu," or "The Battle of the Wood," standing upon a green mound that overlooked the field:

Rush, ye chiefs of the Wood
With the princes in your thousands,
To hinder the hosts of the enemy.

Now the Alders, heading the line,
Thrust forward, the first in time.
The Willows and Mountain Ash
Were late joining the army.
The Blackthorns, full of spines,
And their mate, the Medlar,
Cut down all opposition.
The Rose marched along
Against a hero throng.
The Raspberry was decreed
To serve most usefully as food,
For the sustenance of life—
Not to carry on strife.
The Wild Rose and the Woodbine
With the Ivy intertwined.

How greatly the Poplar trembled,
While much the Cherry dared.
The Birch, for all its ambition,
Was tardily arrayed;
Not from any diffidence, but
Because of its magnificence.
The Laburnum set its heart
On beauty not bravery.
The Yew was to the fore,
At the seat of war.
The Ash was exalted most
Before the sovereign powers.
The Elm, despite vast numbers,
Swerved never a foot,
But fell upon the center,
The wings, and the rear.
The Hazel was esteemed,
By its number in the quiver.
Hail, blessed Cornell tree,
Bull of battle, king of all.
By the channels of the sea,
The Beech did prosperously.
The Holly livid grew,
And manly acts he knew.
The White Thorn checked all—
Its venom scored the palm.
The Vines, which roofed us,
Were cut down in battle
And their clusters plundered.
The Broom, before the rage of war,

In the ditch lay broken.
The Gorse was never prized;
Thus it was vulgarized.
Before the swift Oak darts
Heaven and earth did quake.
The Chestnut suffered shame
At the power of the Yew.

Forest, that caused obstruction,
Thy multitude has been enchanted,
At the Battle of Goddeu Brig.[4]

But, even though the hosts of Gwynedd and Dyfed were thus equal in strength and number to that of Annwn, still they might not prevail because of the nameless one who fought amid his ranks. At length Gwydion, where he rode shoulder to shoulder with Amatheon in the thick of the press, came face to face with a warrior who laid about him in such a manner than none might withstand him for long. Gwydion noticed that he wore in his helm a sprig of Alder, whereupon Gwydion stood straight in his saddle and sang two englyns:

Sure hoofed is my steed impelled by the spur;
The high sprigs of alder are on thy shield;
Bran art thou called, of the glittering branches.

Sure hoofed is my steed in the day of battle:
The high sprigs of alder are in thy hand:
Bran thou art, by the branch thou barest—
Amatheon and Gwydion have thus prevailed.

Was it truly Bran himself who marched in the ranks of Annwn? Even now I cannot say. Certainly, it was not that Bran with whom I had conversed upon the island of Gwales. Yet Annwn is indeed the realm of the dead, among other things, and there was that about the warrior that struck a chord within me. Perhaps he was, like I, forever bound to the Cauldron's rim, so that where it was, so must he follow, as spirit, or dream, or in the form and flesh of another.

Nevertheless, from that moment the host of Annwn began to retreat, while the men of Gwynedd and Dyfed pressed forward, and the army of the trees went with them.

Then Arawn pen Annwn himself rode up to the brothers and sued for peace, for without the power of the Cauldron, and without the secret power of the nameless warrior, he might not prevail.

Thus Amatheon and Gwydion won the day, and not only did they keep the White Roebuck and the Hound of Gwythyr, but they gained the promise of the Lord of Annwn that he would not hunt upon their lands again. And it is said that Arawn demanded angrily to know how they had contrived to hide the name of the man within their host who might not be overcome. Gwydion laughed at this and told him that it was no man at all, but a woman, and since it no longer mattered who knew her name, it was Achren, which means "trees." Arawn was discomfited to hear this because of the way Gwydion, Amatheon, and I had outwitted him with our army of trees, and because *achren* was the word he had put upon the lock that held the White Roebuck and the Hound within his own kingdom.

Thus Arawn came to have an especial hatred towards myself and ever looked to find ways to do me hurt, as shall be told in the story of "The Defense of the Chair."

THE TREE

Time out of mind I watched the tree—
In less than a moment entered its heart.
Dreaming there through the seasons
I felt summer fade with an exhausted sigh.

Wind among the gray boughs
Changed its roaring to a song.
Leaning into it, I laughed
'Till it parched lips and throat.

Autumn fell away behind me
With a gleam of gold under every hedge.
All winter I watched the snowfields,
Saw the sun burn and the moon conquer.

I dreamed and awoke to spring.
Having learned all I might
I went singing away.
In sunlight the tree mourned my song.

10

THE INUNDATION

There have been many tales concerning the sea's war with the Land. The one most people know is that of drowned Atlantis, from which the Old Ones are said to have come. (Perhaps this tale is true, for where else could the power of Merlin or Gwenddydd have sprung?) I remember listening as Trystan wept in the High King's hall over the loss of his own land. But Lyonesses was drowned because of his neglect, for like Gwyddno, the father of the young prince Elffin, Trystan was one of the Sea Kings, who must perform the ceremony of marriage with the Goddess every year lest she take back what is rightly hers.

I had heard of such things before and questioned my master on this point at some length. As I understood what he told me, there was a belief among the ancient people of this Land that just as they must win Sovereignty from the Goddess in whose gift it lay, so must certain lands be kept from the sea by means of propitiation. My master was clear on one point at least—that the sacrifice of men or beasts was not a part of this propitiation, as in some pagan countries.

THE SONG OF TALIESIN ✦ ✦ ✦ ✦

But there is a story that touches more directly upon my own life, as well as the inner life of the Land later ruled over by the High King. This concerns the Cantr'e Gwaelod, or Lowland Hundred, which was the richest part of Gwyddno Garanhir's lands. It was here that the weir was situated, in which, as others have said who know no better, I was found by Prince Elffin. They are wrong, of course, who believe this, but they are right to tell that it was a place of sacred exchange between the Land and the sea, which gave of its plenty every May Eve by filling the weir with enough salmon to make Gwyddno rich for the rest of the year.

I see that you frown, little monk. You also have heard the story of how I was found there, floating in a coracle in a leather bag into which my "Mother"—the Old One herself, the gods forbid!—had laid me before casting me adrift. Thus do the old mysteries become tales, and the tales become twisted out of shape. I was indeed the offspring of the Old One Ceridwen, but not in the way of natural birth. I was her son through the mystery of initiation, which I underwent upon the mountain. After, I floated for a long time out of this world. When I came to rest at length, it was in Gwyddno's land. From thence I became the Bard of the court, and young Elffin became my pupil. I have already told you the story of how I came to rescue him from the old fox Maelgwn.

That story is among those I have gathered here, which I have named "The Road to Deganwy."

The ceremony of marriage with the sea, which Gwyddno was bound to perform, is simple enough to describe. Gwyddno, as her priest, went first to beg water from the priestess of a certain spring that rose a few miles inland. Then, having obtained a cup of this water, he walked the full distance to the sea and went naked into it. There he emptied out the cup of water and cast certain other offerings upon every ninth wave with the appropriate words of invocation. If everything was done correctly, he would reemerge from the sea, and the ceremony was at an end. At one time, I believe, there was more to this; perhaps the lord took a virgin with him into the water and deflowered her. But in the days of which I speak, this practice, if ever it existed, had ceased. Though, as you will see, it may well seem that the thought behind it lingered still in the minds of some.

Now after Elffin's wife Elaint died, the young prince was for a long while inconsolable. But, as is the way with men, in time he began to look about for a new woman, and his eye settled upon one who was named Meroe. She was fair indeed, and of good stock, though her name, which means "of the sea" ought to have warned him of what was to come. Unfortunately for Elffin, Meroe had already been selected to become the next Guardian of the sacred spring, the old one having recently died, which meant that she could never marry but must make herself available to any weary or benighted traveler who passed that way. Also, it was the custom for the king to lie with her when he came to take the offering of water to the sea. In this way the king's virility was proven before he, symbolically, mated with the Goddess herself.

Such rites had been the way in that part of the Land for as long as the memories of the people stretched back. Thus Elffin found himself in love with a girl whom he not only could not marry, but who was soon to be ritually bedded by his own father. But Elffin, who was always headstrong, decided to take matters into his own hands. I knew nothing of his plan, of course, though I should have realized it sooner than I did.

Meroe was installed, with due ceremony, as the new Guardian of the Well. Elffin took to visiting the spring almost every day, though he told no one, least of all me, where he was going or what he did there. He could, of course, by right claim to be a weary or benighted traveler and therefore entitled to the favors of the Guardian, but two things should have barred him from the course he took: his desire for the woman, who was now considered sacred, and his relationship to his father, whose duties he would, one day, take upon himself.

These matters are never easy to explain. You must understand that the relationship of king to Land is a sacred one, and when the bond that is between them is broken, as it was in the High King's day, then disaster inevitably follows. I

THE INUNDATION

suppose you could say that what happened in Cantr'e Gwaelod was, in some way, a prelude and a foreshadowing of the disaster that was to come to the Land as a whole: Arthur's betrayal of the Goddess bringing about the eventual destruction of the realm, which Merlin helped fashion and which I helped protect until I could do so no longer.

Well, the time came for the annual marriage of the Land and the sea. Gwyddno, dressed in his finest robes, went in procession to the spring, where Meroe waited in a robe of white, and the two went into the hut where the Guardian lived. What passed between them cannot be known with any certainty. It is likely that at some point Meroe told Gwyddno about his son, though whether it was before, or after, he tried to bed her, I cannot say. Whatever took place, the outcome was that Gwyddno failed to do what he was supposed to do. He emerged, pale of face, and somehow led the procession from the spring to the sea. He must have decided to brazen it out—foolishly, because he should have known that the Goddess cannot be gulled.

On the way, the weather, which had been fair until that moment, became overcast. A fine rain began to fall as the procession wound its way down to the shore. There, everyone who was well enough to stand was waiting to watch the ceremony. I stood with them, but a notable absence was the King's son. No one had seen Elffin since the morning, when he had ridden off somewhere without a word to anyone. It was assumed that he would reappear in time, and no one was really worried. Despite the rain, it was a cheerful crowd in holiday mood who awaited the arrival of Gwyddno in full expectation that all was well and that everything would follow the usual course.

As the King's party came into sight, announced by cheering from the crowd, a wind blew up from nowhere and began whipping the waves to foam. A cold breath streamed along the beach, and for the first time, people began to look both puzzled and, here and there, apprehensive. I looked at Gwyddno and saw that he was pale and that his smile was fixed, though he carried the cup of well water steadily as ever. I began to search the crowd for a sign of Elffin. When I could not find him, I began to wonder.

The wind rose as Gwyddno's attendants helped him out of his robes. The rain lashed us, the wind thundered around us, and the sea was churned into a millrace of white waves. The crowd—you could not have heard them if they had been still cheering—were utterly silent, as Gwyddno, gritting his teeth visibly to stop them from chattering, though whether from fear or cold could scarcely be said, walked forward into the fury of the breakers.

The sky grew darker as we all waited, straining our eyes through the spuming rain to see the King's broad back and shoulders moving forward steadily into the sea. Perhaps I alone knew the moment when he staggered and fell; for the rest it must have seemed that he was suddenly no longer there. They waited, silent and still, for some time, before heads began to turn, mouths to open and shut, voices to cry out. "What's wrong? What has happened? Where is the King?" I knew by then that Gwyddno was not coming back and began to guess the reason for it. The king in such rites must always be perfect, a man strong in virility as well as purpose. To make the offering in a state less than this was to court disaster.

Then the wind fell, as suddenly as it had risen. The rain cleared, and the sea fell back to its normal steady rhythm. All eyes focused on the place where Gwyddno had vanished. Not so much as a ripple broke the surface. It was as if the King had never existed. Then a cry went up. Someone had spotted a lone figure walking slowly along the shore towards us. It was Elffin. As he drew near, the crowd parted to give him passage. He walked on until he stood on the very edge of the sea, with the waves licking at his boots.

I thought for a moment that he was going to follow his father into the waves, but instead he bent down to retrieve something from the water. It was the great silver and gold cup that had been used to carry the water of the sacred well. The Goddess had taken the offering, and more beside, returned the vessel empty.

Slowly, head bent, Elffin turned his back on the sea and walked towards Caer Cenedir. After a moment, I followed and felt the crowd, still too stunned by what had occurred to speak or think, follow in turn.

The year that followed was a bad one. Crops failed, and the fishing was poor. A number of women died in childbed, and several children sickened and died without apparent reason. It was evident that the Goddess was angry, though no one could understand why. Most blamed Gwyddno for some inexplicable and unknowable crime that had demanded his sacrifice, but they wondered at the same time why his death had not propitiated the Goddess. I alone guessed Elffin's secret, though when I tried to get him to speak of it, I met with stony silence. He took his father's place without contest and did what he could to succor those who suffered hardship. Whether he went still to the sacred well or avoided Meroe as the cause of his father's death, I chose not to know.

Then came Seithenin.

He was the warden of the great dike that ran inland from the seawall for more than fifty leagues across the border of Cantr'e Gwaelod and kept the sea at bay. He was also cousin to Gwyddno and his trusted counselor. I suppose he expected to fulfill the same function for Elffin. Also, I believe, he was not adverse to trying to gain something from the events of May Eve. There were many who thought him better fitted to rule than Elffin, whose old reputation as a man with bad luck began to be revived at this time. I did what I could by way of reassurance, but found, not for the first time, that I was myself the subject of fear and distrust. People remembered how I was found and the way in which I had entered the Prince's service.

Seithenin was quick to realize this and to make as much of it as he could. I began to see people making the sign against evil when they thought I was not looking, and though this gave me some amusement, I understood well enough what it meant.

How matters would have come out in the end is difficult to say. In all likelihood, Seithenin would have taken the throne away from Elffin, and I would have been forced to flee. But an event occurred that put even Gwyddno's strange death into shadow.

Seithenin visited the Sacred Well. That in itself was no strange thing for him to do. It was what he did there that broke every law in the Land. He raped the Guardian of the Well.

Seithenin must have seen Meroe before and desired her. At least, that is the most obvious reason, though others are possible. Also, on that occasion, he was drunk. Drink was, perhaps, his one weakness, for in other ways, he was a good man by most accounts: strong, wily and, at least until Gwyddno's death, loyal. Whatever the reason, whatever excuse might be made or unmade, the facts are unchangeable. Seithenin raped the Guardian of the Well, she whose task it was to gratify the needs of travelers and wayfarers and who stood as representative of the Goddess in Cantr'e Gwaelod.

Such an act could not go unpunished, nor would it. But the first that anyone knew of it was when a storm broke of such violence that no one living could remember its like. It made the storm that had taken Gwyddno seem a shower of summer rain, and everyone knew at once that a tempest of this magnitude betokened evil. Then, a man arrived, wild-eyed and bedraggled, with news that set every heart quaking: The seawall had been breached.

There was scarcely a man, woman, or child who did not know what this meant. Unless a miracle occurred, Cantr'e Gwaelod was doomed. The seawall was all that kept the hungry waters out of the Lowland; without it, the whole Cantr'e would be under water in a matter of hours.

Elffin, pale but steady, sent men to find out how bad the breach was and if anything could be done to repair it. He also prepared a message to be taken to the Guardian of the Well, petitioning for the judgment of the Goddess. This remedy had not been employed in a hundred years, but it was known that it could be used in circumstances of gravest need. Elffin chose me to take the message, and though I saw some uncertain looks among the courtiers, it seemed that I was still considered the best choice.

I saddled my horse and rode through a screaming gale to the Well. There I found the evidence of Seithenin's handiwork. The hut where the Guardian lived was broken, and amid its ruins, I found the body of Meroe. It looked as though she had taken her own life, though it was hard to be certain. Of Seithenin there was no sign.

I knelt amid the ruins of the place and tried to understand what was required of me. With the wisdom of the Cauldron I knew there was only one solution, though it grieved me to think of it. I took the great cup, which had somehow escaped the struggle that had taken place there, and filled it with water from the Well. I half-expected to be struck down for doing so, but nothing happened. The storm continued to howl around me, but it grew no worse.

I rode back as fast as I could to Caer Cenedir and, slipping into the hall as quietly as I could, broke the news to Elffin of what I had found. Then I gave him the cup. He took it without a word, setting it on the table before him. Then he bent his head and wept bitterly, though whether for himself or his father or the woman he had loved, I know not. After that he took up the cup and walked with it out into the night. Everywhere confusion reigned, as families fled the Caer and sought higher ground. The report from the seawall was bad; it had been breached in three places, and the sea was pouring through, whipped to even greater fury by the storm. For a long time no one noticed that the King was gone.

That night is one that I remember still. There are times when I awake to hear the sound of wind and rain screaming against each other like great beasts, and I am back again in Cenedir on that fearful night. At such times I remember Elffin and Gwyddno and the land of Cantr'e Gwaelod. But above all I remember the hungry cry of the sea as it devoured the land.

Like everyone else, I took horse and rode inland, seeking safer ground. I found people all along the way, huddling for shelter beneath trees or bushes or simply standing, hock-deep in mud, staring at nothing, having given up all attempt to go farther.

By morning the storm had blown itself out. The sea lay flat calm, glinting in the pale morning sun. But most of Cantr'e Gwaelod lay under it, drowned forever beneath the restless waves.[1] Caer Cenedir was gone, washed away as if it had never existed. Hundreds of men, women, and children had been lost; the few who survived huddled miserably together with the blank haunted looks of those who have suffered a disaster beyond their comprehension.

Gradually the full extent of the inundation grew clearer. Many leagues of land, most, indeed, of the Lowland Hundred, lay under water. Overnight the Cantr'e had virtually ceased to exist. Farther along the coast Gwyddno Garanhir's weir still stood, and there, a few days later, the body of Elffin was found, white and bloated as a dead fish. Thus he came ashore again, just as I was said to have done, save that he had no gift of poems, no magical message for the world.

I did not weep for Elffin. He had brought upon himself the disaster that had consumed him and all his kin. I saw, too, the work of the Goddess in this, for she could be pitiless indeed to those who broke faith with her, as assuredly both Gwyddno and later Elffin did, each in his own way. Of Seithenin no more was heard, and it was assumed that he had drowned along with the rest. Certainly I hope it was so, for if his end was otherwise, it must have been dreadful indeed.

Afterwards, before I left the drowned land forever, I made this song:

Seithenin, stand thou forth
And behold the billowy waves.
The sea has covered Gwyddno's lands.

Remembered be the maiden
Who, after conflict, let loose
The fountain of the Goddess, the desolate sea.

The cry of Meroe rises to the heavens;
Today even the gods do not hear.
Common after excess comes restraint.

A cry from the sea overpowers me tonight,
It is not easy to relieve me.
Common after excess is adversity.

A cry from the sea comes on the wind;
The mighty and beneficent one has caused it.
Common after excess is want.

A cry from the roaring sea
Impels me from my resting place this night;
Common after excess is great destruction.

The grave of Seithenin, the weak-minded,
Between Caer Cenedir and the shore
Is lost beneath the great sea forever.

THE LOST LIGHT

Cold and smooth as polished bone
the dream flew in the poet's head.
He seized at the edge of meaning
bobbing on the rim of his thought;
he heard, like a distant cry of birds,
the reechoed memory of his truth.

Darkly he walked on the hills' back
piping like a hedgefull of birds.
Spread his arms like wings
and caught the sun between them.
Squeezing it in his two hands,
he tossed it back into the sky,

went laughing on his way.

11

AMAIRGEN'S STORY

here have been many great poets in the Island of the Mighty and in the Land of Eriu across the little sea. I am but the last in a line of Bards, trained in the ways of the Wood and the Cauldron, taught to read the book of the past and the mirror of the future, and to walk between the worlds at will. ❧ Of all those who are named in the books of lore as mighty and deeply perceiving poets, one stands out above them all. Wherever folk gather to talk of the ancient wisdom, the name of Amairgen is spoken, his words quoted, his songs recited. Yet, few there are now living who remember the story I am about to tell. It has been forgotten in the world these many years; in the Wood, where all such things are remembered, it is told still. Therefore, I will tell it now, so that you, little monk, may set it down so that others, who come after, may read it and understand, if they wish, what makes a true poet. ❧ This was the way of it. ❧ There was once in Ulster a great smith named Eccet,[1] but though that was his given name, he was more often called Salach, which means, in the Irish tongue, "The Sooty"—a good enough name for one who plies the craft of smithering. And, lest this be forgotten also in the passage of time, be sure that you set down that the office of smith has always been recognized as sacred, his knowledge of things Other being great due to his mastery of the element of fire. From Goibhniu to Wayland,[2] there have been smiths who were more than half gods, and though Eccet (or Salach) was of human stock, there was more than a little of the Otherworld about him, though I would say that the same is true for most men of Ireland I have known.

Anyway, Eccet had two children, a boy and a girl. Their mother was of faery stock and died in bearing them. For which reason, as is often the way, Eccet gave them less attention and love than he might. Though the girl grew up well enough, the boy, Amairgen, was a strange child, who spoke to no one and kept himself to himself, spending most of his days sitting by the fire in the smithy, watching the coals glow red as his father worked the bellows and beat out the song of all smiths on his anvil.

Thus matters stood until the boy was fourteen years old. Most thought him half-witted, for he was unlovely to look upon, his skin blackened and cracked from sitting close to the fire, and he was always silent, from which it was deemed either that he could not speak or that his brain was too addled to fit words together.

Now in another part of Ulster lived the master poet Aitherne, who was rightly judged the greatest of his kind in all of Ireland, and maybe in the Island of the Mighty itself. But great though he was, he was also proud and cruel by nature and used his skills to better himself at the expense of others.

One day Aitherne happened to send his servant, Greth, on an errand to Eccet's smithy. There Greth happened to see the smith's two children: the girl, radiant as a sun mote; the boy, dirty, hunched, and silent at her feet. As he waited for Eccet to finish the task for his master, the boy, who had never been known to speak, looked directly at Greth and said, "Ask your master if he eats curds and slops, as I do, or if he has eaten of the Salmon of Wisdom. For I am sick of the food of men and would sup at the table of poetry."

The servant was so terrified at being spoken to in this manner by a child who had never until that day spoken that he fled home and told Aitherne everything. The master poet at once grew silent and grim, for he knew from the words the youth had uttered that he would one day be an even greater poet than he, and this he feared greatly, lest his own power be challenged.

When Eccet heard that his son had spoken for the first time, and furthermore in a manner that none might clearly understand, and to whom he had spoken, he saw at once that Amairgen was in great danger from Aitherne. Therefore he set to work with what skills he himself possessed to save the boy from certain destruction.

To Amairgen's sister he said, "You must take your brother away from here at once. Prepare yourself for a long journey." Then, while the girl, wide-eyed, did as she was bid, Eccet shut himself in the smithy and, with the craft and cunning of his kind, set to work to make a simulacrum of Amairgen. He took earth and spittle and molded them roughly into the form he desired. Then, heating the forge, he took a single coal, breathed upon it, dropped a little of his blood onto it, and placed it in the breast of the image.

In a little while, there lay by the fire, as though deeply asleep, a shape like that of Amairgen, while the real youth was put upon a horse and carried away by his sister, who had instructions to take him to her mother's folk, the people of the Sidhe. Eccet had searched his heart deeply before he chose this refuge for his son, for since the death of his wife, he had closed his heart to all who came of the Otherworld and set powerful wards around his dwelling to keep all such from his door. Now he sent with his two children tokens, given to him long since by their mother, that he knew would gain them admittance to the Hollow Hills.

Meanwhile, Aitherne came to the smithy, grumbling about his foolish servant and requesting the work that Eccet had been completing for him. Though he smiled outwardly, in his heart there was blackness. When he saw where the image of Amairgen lay, apparently asleep by the fire, he drew forth a knife that he had concealed beneath his robe, and while Eccet was out of the room, stabbed the boy in the heart and fled. In his fury and arrogance, he had failed to see that the child was but an image of earth and fire.

Of course, Eccet set up a great outcry and went to the Brehons (judges) in search of restitution. He made sure that part of the eric (honor price) that Aitherne had to pay by way of restitution included the promise to foster "a son" of the smith and train him in the arts of poetry until he was as much a master as Aitherne himself. To this pledge the master poet agreed, though in his heart he felt certain that, by the time Eccet had another son of sufficient age to become his pupil, there would be none who cared to enforce the eric.

In the meantime, Amairgen and his sister had found shelter in the Sidhe near Sleive Mis, in the south of Ulster. There the sooty youth began to show his worth, for it seemed that in all the years of silent watching, he had learned all that the fire had to tell, and that learning had made him a poet indeed, with all the skills beside of a shaman.[3]

Thus Amairgen remained within the Hollow Hills and learned there much wisdom, including the mastery of the elements, the secret language of poets,[4] the arts of shape-shifting, and the mysteries of star lore, such as the ancient folk knew better than anyone in the lands above.

In due time, Amairgen grew from child to youth, and at that time, he left the Sidhe and returned to his father's house. Eccet then went to Aitherne and demanded payment in full of the eric, that he should now take his son and train him to be a master poet. To this, Aitherne had to agree, though he did so with ill grace. Still, he had no knowledge that the youth now presented to him was Amairgen, for, during his sojourn in the realm below, the "sooty" child had vanished forever, and in his place stood a tall, handsome youth with the light of the stars upon his brow.

Still, being a man filled with wisdom and cunning, Aitherne decided to test his new pupil by setting him to prepare the belly of a pig for the cauldron. (From this you may see, little monk, that there are patterns in the training of poets that are repeated, for was I not also set to watch a Cauldron, and was not Finn given a fish to cook?)[5]

Amairgen set to work with a will. After he had watched him for a time, Aitherne spoke to him in the speech of the initiates, which only master poets may understand. He said, "*Dofotha tairr tein,*" which means, "It is time to take it off the fire." At once Amairgen replied, "*Toe lethaig foem friss ocus fris adaind,*" which is to say, "Put a kneading trough under the meat and light a candle to see if the belly is truly boiled."[6]

Then Aitherne was astonished and asked Amairgen some further questions and, within the space of an hour, declared that there was nothing further that he could teach the youth. So humbled was he that he prepared to retire to a solitary place for the rest of his days. But then the youth showed how great was his magnanimity and wisdom, for he declared that Aitherne was still due the respect of a master poet, and that it had been decided long since that Aitherne would be his tutor. Then he revealed his identity and forgave the older man wholeheartedly. At this, Aitherne wept, tore his poet's robe, and said that he was ashamed of his prideful nature. Thereafter, it is said, he became a changed man, while Amairgen, as is told in the books of lore, became the greatest poet in the whole of Eriu at that time.

Thus do I, Taliesin pen Beirdd, Chief Poet of the Island of the Mighty, greet one who was a great master, and if I, too, have suffered from overweening pride, may I learn humility in my time.

*T*hough *my master was indeed a proud man, yet I saw how that pride was tempered by justice and wisdom, which only those who have suffered in the world may acquire. For he was, in his way, as kind and generous of spirit as any man I ever knew.*

IN WINTER'S SHADOW

Under the brow of winter
Taliesin stood,
Feeling, in head and heart,
The tremor of ice-kept streams.
His eyes were the color of ice.

Watching, from sheltering stones,
He felt, in hands and feet,
The pain of snow-bound boughs.
His eyes were the color of frost.
Then, as snow flowed from him,
His voice thawed.
He barked like a fox at midnight,
Sang with the waters' release.
His eyes were the color of spray.

12

THE CONTENTION OF LLUD AND LLEVELYS

There are many stories concerning the Sovereignty of the Island of the Mighty, but none more strange than that of Llud and Llevelys. These two were brothers, sons of Beli Mawr, who was king over all Britain in a distant time, before even the Old Ones walked the Land. Of the many dreams I had from the Cauldron, this tale seems to me one that had more meaning for the time of the Pendragons than any other.[1] ❧ This was the way of it. ❧ After the death of Beli Mawr, Llud became king, and for a time, he ruled wisely and well, and the Land was without strife. Then one day, when he and Llevelys were together at Llud's chief place and both looking at the night sky, a strange mood came upon them. "See," said Llud, "what an extensive field I possess." ❧ "Where is it?" asked Llevelys. ❧ Llud pointed at the heavens, which stretched in a great canopy overhead. ❧ Llevelys smiled and said, "Ah, brother, but see how many sheep and cattle I have grazing in your field." ❧ "Where are they?" asked Llud. ❧ "Why, there," replied Llevelys, pointing at the heavens. "See? The great host of stars, each one of golden brightness, and the moon their shepherd."

Llud's face grew dark with anger. "They shall not graze on my field," he said, and with that, he struck his brother.

So it came about that the two brothers quarreled bitterly. This ended in Llevelys being sent away, out of the Land of Britain, to seek sanctuary, for Llud let it be known that if any man saw his brother on the road, he was to kill him.

So things stood for a time. But then Llud decided to take a queen. The woman he chose was Gwyar, the daughter of a neighboring king named Rhitta Gawr who had, unbeknownst to Llud, some skill with magic and enchantment. Now Rhitta, who was a greedy man as well as a powerful enchanter, had long desired to replace Llud as the High King of all Britain. He persuaded his daughter that if she could weaken her husband in his rule, she and her father would reap great benefit. This she set out to do, preying ever upon Llud's mind with little spiteful thoughts and words, though always concealed in fair speech and accompanied by smiles rather than frowns. As a result, Llud grew ever grimmer and more ill at ease.

From that time, things went ill with the Land. For two years in succession, the crops failed, and on every side men began to murmur against Llud. Then the Land was visited by three plagues, which came from none knew where. The first was in the form of a people named the Corannyied, who settled like locusts upon the Land, and wherever they came, the Land dried up, so that nothing grew there. The second was a dreadful shout that carried across the length and breadth of the Land, and when it was heard, women miscarried, men lost their strength, and animals fell dead. The third plague was that no matter what provisions Llud prepared for his people in the evening, by the next day, they were consumed by unknown means, though no one saw anything of those who took them.

Thus matters stood for the space of three moons, until Llud was nearly mad with the troubles that beset him. All the while Gwyar whispered in his ear that the plagues were the work of Llevelys, who had surely summoned the help of the Korrigans, the People of the Sea, and sent the plagues to bring down his brother

THE FIELD OF STARS

so that he could rule in his stead. At first, Llud was disbelieving, for at heart he sorely missed his brother, but as the plagues continued, he began to listen to the words of the Queen. At length he sent a message to Llevelys asking him to return to put aside their old quarrel. But in truth he intended to cast his brother into the deepest prison, until either the plagues ceased, or Llevelys died, whichever was the sooner.

But Gwyar came to Llud and spoke of a dream she had had in which it was revealed to her that if Llevelys was slain, and his blood spilled upon the earth, the plagues would cease, and all would be well with the Land. In his desperation, Llud listened to her and believed her, though in his heart he knew the falseness of her words.

When Llevelys arrived, for he willingly answered his brother's call, he was at once seized and bound, and Llud's Druids prepared to let out his life on the Land. Llevelys begged that he might see his brother once again, and that if this wish were granted, he would willingly give up his life. Because it was known that a willing sacrifice is always more effective, Llud agreed to see Llevelys, despite the advice of the Queen, who feared that her plotting would be thus discovered.

When the two brothers were together, Llevelys said, "Brother, I know of the plagues that have troubled you, and I know how they may be banished. For truly they are none of my doing but are the work of another. In the name of our common blood, will you allow me to tell you how to be rid of these things?"

To this Llud agreed at once; nor would he be swayed from his intent, for when he saw his brother stand before him, the lies with which Gwyar had filled his ears sounded false and thin. Llevelys told him to send out men to catch certain insects, bring them to the court, and have them pounded together in water. Then, when this was done, he should call all the people of his tribe and those of the Corannyied together, on the pretext of making peace between them. When they were gathered, he should cause the water in which the insects were mixed to be thrown over the whole company. "For," Llevelys said, "when this is done, the Corannyied will depart and trouble you no more."

All was done as Llevelys instructed, and all fell out exactly as he predicted. The moment the water touched the Corannyied, they shrieked and fled. Some say that they became insects themselves and flew away.

Then Llevelys was brought before Llud again and told him how to be rid of the second plague. "The shriek," he said, "comes from the noise of two great boars, who fight every day at noon. You must find the place where they dwell, which is at the very center of the Land, and there dig a pit. In the pit you should put a great vat of mead, covered over with a thickly woven cloth. When the pigs smell the drink, they will leap upon the cloth and sink to the bottom of the vat, where they will drink all the mead. When they have done so, they will fall into a deep sleep, and while they are sleeping, you must capture them, put them into a stone chest, and bury them in a deep pit. So long as they are buried, no further harm will come to the Land."

Once again, all was done as Llevelys required; and once again, all fell out exactly as he had predicted. Some who tell this story would have it that the pigs were dragons, but they have grown confused from hearing of how Merlin discovered two such creatures beneath the hill of Dinas Emrys. That event is part of the story of the Pendragons[2] and had no part in the matter of Llud and Llevelys.[3]

Once again the prisoner was brought forth, and this time he asked that he might speak to Llud alone, which the King granted. When the brothers were alone, Llevelys grasped Llud by the hand and said, "Brother, I have rid you of two of the plagues, but the third will be the most difficult. For it is a great and terrible creature that consumes your provisions each night. Strong and cunning it is, and invisible to all who are not prepared in a certain way. But tonight, if you do as I shall advise, you will catch the creature at its work and destroy it." Then he gave Llud the juice of a certain flower with which to anoint his eyelids and counseled him to say nothing of what had passed between them, for a reason that would later become clear.

As Llevelys had instructed, Llud pretended that he could not understand the words his brother had spoken concerning the third plague and ordered him to be imprisoned again. But that night he anointed his eyelids and lay in wait for the creature. Sure enough, towards the middle of the night, he saw a huge, misshapen form enter the hall. It was taller than a man, and its arms all but touched the ground, with great claws on them like knives. Its head was somewhat like that of a dragon, with cruel jaws and eyes as red as jewels. A smell came from it as of something that had been living at the bottom of a lake for many ages.

At once, the creature began to consume the food that had been set out for the people of the castle, and in a few moments, it had devoured sufficient to feed a hundred men for a week. All around, the men who had been set to guard the provisions stood, or sat, or slept, unable to see what was happening. But Llud, who could see everything, drew his sword and sprang out upon the beast.

Soon people came running to see what was causing the commotion. They stared in astonishment at the sight of their lord, apparently fighting with himself, until with a great cry, he drove his sword deep into the creature's heart, so that it fell twitching on the ground. In that moment, the monster became visible to all.

Then an even stranger thing happened. For a moment the creature lay where it had fallen. Then its form grew blurred, and in its place lay the body of a man. It was someone that all there recognized, for the body on the ground belonged to Rhitta Gawr, the father of Llud's Queen. Gwyar herself gave a cry of anguish as she saw it and fell in a faint.

Llevelys then came forward and said, "Thus is the last of the plagues brought to an end. And it was indeed your wife, Queen Gwyar, and her father Rhitta Gawr, who lies dead before you, who were the cause of all this misery. Rhitta it was who invited the Corannyied here with promises of rich lands to suck dry; and he it was who set free the sacred swine from their captivity, so that they might ravage the Land. And Rhitta, as you see, was the beast who consumed the provisions for your men. What now do you say to my own part in this? Am I innocent or guilty?"

With one accord Llevelys was declared innocent and released. But as for Queen Gwyar, for the evil she had done, Llud declared her guilty, and she was taken out immediately and killed, and her blood scattered upon the Land. When this was done, all those places that had become desolate because of the Corannyied grew green again.

Thus were the three plagues ended, and thus the quarrel between Llud and Llevelys mended. Never again did the brothers look at the sky and boast of their riches, and thus the Land flowered and bore fruit once more.

All this happened long ago, and who is to say if it be true or not? But this much I know: the Land must be well served by its kings, or else it will turn against them. More, where two brothers share the custody of the Land, if there is bad blood between them, then surely ill tidings will follow.

I, Taliesin, have told it.

THE RAID ON ANNWN

I

The acorn cup is filled with blood
And starlight trembles
In the mirror of Annwn.

Downward the Director of Toil
Led us, and we followed,
Into the shadow of the shadow,
And beyond, into
The full weight of Winter,
Iron armor of ice
That kept us slow.

Afloat on the Dragon-raft
We approached sunset, the tower
Where night's agents flamed.
We followed our lord
To the night of midnight
Where even Time's sickness
Can be cured.

II

Ocean showed us the way
towards sun and after-sun.

Trailing our bow through light
the way fell into mid-world.

Mirrored by stars we watched

the slow revolving of spheres.

At last, in comprehension,
not lost, we spoke the Name.

It sang, swordlike,
in the dark. Waking

In the mouth of Annwn
the lap of water and the creak of oars.

III

What wind blows in Annwn?
How are the sails of Prydwen filled?
On the Dragon's breath we sailed
Towards the rim of the world.
Beneath the head of the Beast
Were stars for scales . . .
The clatter of his breath
Rang in our ears;
Our eyes, filled with shadows,
Mirrored stars.

The maze dissolved
In shards of sun;
And water drew back
From the lip of shore.
Sailing in, the lantern
Swayed in the wind;
Returning, the flame
Stands still as a spear.

13

THE CROW, THE SALMON, AND THE OLDEST OF THE OLD

any days and nights we labored in the little hut in the mountains: I to copy the stories my master Taliesin told me; he to search his memory for the things he deemed important enough to relate. One such day, in the dead of winter, I happened to remark that I could not remember a night as cold as this in all my life. Taliesin smiled at that and replied that he knew one that was far more bitter, and that he had heard of it from the oldest living creature. Then he told me this story, which I have set down as faithfully as I can.

n the days when my name was still Gwion and I was the servant of the Old One, I saw many strange things that even now seem more like dreams than reality—indeed, perhaps they were dreams, sent to me as part of the training and preparation I had to undergo before I was ready to drink the brew of the Cauldron. ❧ One time I was crouching in the corner of the Old One's malodorous hut, keeping as silent and still as possible to avoid drawing attention to myself, when I heard a scrabbling at

143

the door. Herself, whom I still hesitate to name even now that I am far from her influence, got up from where she sat, muttering, by the fire and opened the door. Outside was a crow, so bedraggled and battered by the elements as to be scarcely recognizable. It hopped across the door sill and croaked at the Old One—save that from where I sat, the sounds I heard issuing from its bill were words of human speech, though I had not then learned the speech of bird and beast, nor the art of shifting my form to that of any creature of the air, water, or land.

*S*uch statements as this I learned to accept, though they caused my flesh to shudder and the hairs on my body to stand out.

Thus I was party to the following dialogue, which you will say is fancy, little monk, but which I say teaches all and more than one could wish to know about the nature of this world.[1]

First I heard the crow say: "So cold it is, and long has been my journey! Nights and nights ago, I spoke with the Eagle of Leithin and asked her if she could ever remember a time when it was this cold. She answered that never in her long life could she remember anything to equal it. But she said that there were those who would remember.

"'And who are they?' I asked her, to which she replied that I should visit Dubhschosach, the Black-Footed Stag of Ben Gulban, who was as old as the Deluge.[2]

"I set forth at once to find the stag, though I can scarce speak of the trial it was, for so great was the cold, that ice formed upon my wings as I flew, and it took me days to reach Ben Gulban. But at last I sighted the stag, standing in the snow, rubbing his back against the stump of an ancient oak.

"Again I asked the question I had asked of the Eagle, whether he remembered a time as cold as this, to which he gave answer that never had he seen anything to equal it. When I asked his age, to gauge how long he could remember, he showed me the oak stump and said: 'I was born beneath that tree when it was but a sapling. I watched it grow into the mightiest of oaks, and ever I used to come to rub myself against its side. Now it is the merest stump that you see, for I have quite worn it away with my rubbing. But in all that time I never saw a night as cold as this last night.' Thus the Stag spoke, who then told me that if I would speak with one even older than he, I should seek out Dubhgoire, the Blackbird of Clonfert, who was said to be wise beyond the knowledge of all created things."

The crow paused in its narrative and panted for a while. The Old One, in an unusual display of feeling, fetched it water to drink. Then the wonderful recital continued, and still I listened from my dark corner, eager to learn all that I might.

"So," said the bird, when it had drunk its fill and began to fluff out its draggled feathers, "I flew by night and by day, against storms such as no living creature recalled, to Clonfert, and there I met the Blackbird, who was as large as a swan, but sleek and dark as black blood. I asked her if she remembered such a time as that which we were now experiencing. But Dubhgoire shook her head. 'Three hundred years have I lived in this place, and before that, three hundred more in another place, but never, in all that time, have I known the like of this cold. But there is one older than I, who may have the knowledge you seek. Go to Assaroe and speak to the Salmon who lives in the pool there. Gol is he called, for he has but a single eye. He, perhaps, will know what you seek.'[3]

"And so I set out again, and there is no telling the hardships I endured. But at length I reached Assaroe and saw the lake where the old, blind Salmon was believed to live. I searched for him all that day until I saw his shadowy shape in the water and flew down to question him. Again I asked if his memory reached back far enough to say whether he had ever known a day as cold as that which had just passed.

"Gol answered, 'I am so old that I remember the coming of the Fir Bolg,[4] and I remember how after them came Partholon, and the Tuatha de Danaan, and the Fomorians. I even remember the coming of Fintan. And one day, let me tell you, I remember a time so cold that when I leapt from the water after a beautiful, rainbow fly, the water froze over before I could dive back into it. As I lay there on the ice, flopping and panting, a bird of prey flew down, and when it flew away, it carried with it my one good blue eye, with which I could see all the world. It was only blood pouring from the wound in my head that melted the ice and allowed me to escape again into the water. That was surely the worst day of any that were on this earth. But there is one who knows even better than I if this be true or not, and that is the Oldest of the Old. She lives in the hut beside Lake Tegid in Wales, and if you seek her out, she will certainly tell you if there was ever a worse day than this one that has just gone.'

"And so," said the Crow, "I have come, and I ask the question again. Was there ever a colder day, or a worse, than that which has just lately passed?"

The Old One—and now you may see how well she is named—looked thoughtful for a time. Then she glanced at the crow, which looked a deal less sorry for itself than when it had first entered the hut, and she said, "I will tell you two things. First, I was the bird that took away the eye of Gol the Salmon, for he was becoming too wise for his own good and the good of the right ordering of things. And the second thing is that I do remember a day more cold than that which has just lately passed, and it was that very day of which I speak. Though Gol has spent many years in the shape of a salmon, he was not always so. Sometimes he went as a man upon two legs, and sometimes he was himself a bird—one much like you yourself!"

With that, the Old One threw something that she had been holding all the while in her hands over the head of the crow. It looked like a plaited strand of grass to my eyes, but I know now that it was what is called "a Druid's wisp," a device that can turn men to madness or hold them prisoner.[5] Such I saw was the case this time, for though the crow screeched and tried to fly upwards, it was prevented from doing so by the wisp.

For a moment the shape of the bird grew blurred, and in its place I thought I saw for a moment another—that of a tall man, whose silver hair spread out from his head like a curtain of fine white water. But as swiftly as I thought I saw this, there was only a dusty black crow standing there again on the Old One's table.

She put forth one long, white hand and lifted the bird with surprising gentleness. Carefully she peered at it, then said, "We have played this game too long, you and I. Go back to your lake, old fish, and remain there. The time of reckoning will come, be sure of that." Then moving to the door, she lifted her hand and flung the crow into the air. It flapped and shrieked at her for a moment, then flew off towards the west.

The Old One came back into the hut and seemed for the first time to become aware of me. "I see you, Gwion of the listening ears," she said. "Let me warn you never to let the day dawn when you know too much for your own good." Then she cuffed me and went off about her own business.

I have already told the story of what happened between us when I did indeed come to know more than she deemed fitting. From that time until now she has haunted me through every ward of the Wood, until I am free of her at last.

As for the crow, at a later time I learned his identity. He was indeed Tegid Foel, who had once shared the power of the Cauldron with the Old One herself. What strange rivalry had caused them to become adversaries I know not, nor how he came to be living in the shape of a crow in the mountains. Such things are lost in mists too deep even for me to penetrate. Indeed, I believe there is a bond between them still, and that these games they played were of a kind that we cannot understand.[6]

I do not, truly, know what my master meant by this.

And, such is the circular way of the wood that, as Fionn, I may well have met the old Salmon again and seen his death. But even I cannot say whether that is so or not. But I made a chant of what I heard that day. It goes thus:

> *The age of the ages in triads were told:*
> *Three years the duration of the Alder Pole.*
> *Three times the duration of an Alder Pole,*

The life of a crow in the green wood.
Three times the life of the crow,
The life of a man—a short existence!
Three times the life of a man,
The life of an eagle on the mountain.
Three times the life of an eagle,
The life of a stag in the valleys.
Three times the life of a stag,
The life of a melodious blackbird.
Three times the life of a blackbird
Is that of the Salmon in the lake of Assaroe.
Three times the age of Gol the Wise
Is that of the Old One with her Cauldron.
Only the earth is older than that—
Thrice the age of the Old One
Is the age of the earth.[7]

THE VOICES IN THE GRASS

Taliesin walked where the gray stones rose.
The dry susurration of grass from every side
Sang in the poet's ears as he walked
Recalling the glory of the place whose bones lay bare.
Softly, as the sun beat down,
he heard the Voice of the grass
whispering broken syllables of forgotten speech.
Behind the murmur he heard one voice say:
"Taliesin: Poet, watcher under moon and sun,
Walks where the gray stones once stood tall,
Listens to the voices in the Summer grass,
Remembers the lost time he knew between the walls,
Scents again the perfume of a full-blown rose . . .
Taliesin: Poet, watcher under sun and moon,
Walks where the dry stones . . ."
                                Shrill, the poet
Whistled in the dry air, halting in its tracks
The wild life of the place—while the grass
For a moment seemed to still,
And the Voice he knew as echoing his own
Fell silent among the tumbled stones of Camelot.

14

THE FALL OF THE GREAT TREES

In the beginning of the world, the One Great Tree grew with its roots deep in the wells of the Underworld and its branches among the Summer Stars.[1] Beneath it, the first kings were made, and much of their power was stored within its mighty trunk. Only the greatest of shamans could climb it, from where, looking out from its branching bole, they could see to the very ends of the earth, or even, it is said, find their way between the worlds, returning with word of such places that were but dreams in the minds of other men. ❧ Later, many ages after, the One Great Tree fell—cut down, it is said, by one who sought to destroy the Three Worlds.[2] But even so, it could not be destroyed, so great was the power of the Shaper of Worlds within it. From its wood were made the seven chairs in which sat the Guardians of the Island of the Mighty. The last of these is the chair in which, since the departure of Merlin, I have sat—at times uncomfortably, perhaps. From it I guard and protect the Tree of the Pendragons—for you must know that there are those who would cut it down, even now, and thus destroy much that Arthur built with the aid of the Fellowship of the Table.[3]

I know this statement to be only too true, for there are ever those who would wipe out good and replace it with evil. Even in this sheltered place where I have spent my days since the departure of my Lord Taliesin, rumors have reached me out of the dark. Somewhere, I must believe, the Great Tree of which he spoke, and which, in some way unfathomable to myself, contains the power of the Pendragons, stands still, and is in some way guarded, if no longer by my master, then by some new Guardian who sits in the Chair of Prydein.

From a scion of that first Great Tree grew the woods that went into the making of the Wheel of Taranis,[4] and thus from its ancient, sacred trunk came the letters that Ogma Sun-Face found and from which he discovered the secret language of the poets. From the twigs of that first Great Tree grew the heart of the Wood itself, Broceliande, the forest in which all that I have told, here and elsewhere, took place.

Just as every Land has its Great Tree, so every Great Tree has its Guardian, usually a poet, since it is the poets who have ever possessed the wisdom and understanding necessary for the making of kings.[5] Indeed it is said: Who but a poet may cry aloud the name of the king at the *do gairm rig*, the proclaiming of the king?

But I would speak now of the Great Trees that once stood in Eriu. And I would tell of their fall, and of the circumstances by which that came about, and what that deed meant to Eriu.

First, you must know that, in ancient times, there were five Great Trees in Eriu: the Oak of Mugna, the Yew of Ross, the Bile Tortan, the Bile Dathi, and Craeb Uisnig.[6] Each stood at the center of one of the five districts into which Eriu was divided. At the center of all, in the county of Meath, stood Eo Mugna, the Great Oak, which was a door between the worlds and which held the sacred power of the *Ard Ri*, the Great King, within it. The story of the coming of that tree is told more fully in the tale known as "The Settling of the Manor of Tara." It is too long to tell here, and besides, it has been set down by others, but one part of it I must relate, in order that the story of the fall of the Great Trees may be properly understood along with the message of their passing for the Island of the Mighty.

It was in the time of Dairmuid mac Cerball that the nobles of the other comotes (divisions of land) of Eriu began to murmur against the extent of the lands in the lordship of Tara. When he heard this, Dairmuid called the nobles together and summoned the wisest men in the Land to discuss the matter. From every side came those who were judged wise and who knew the history of the Land for hundreds of years past. But one among them was deemed wiser than all the rest, and that was Fintan, of whom I have spoken before.[7] He had lived for almost as long as men could remember and knew all there was to know of the history of the Invasions and of the different lordships and lands that were in Eriu.

Now, when it came to the matter at hand, Fintan deliberated for a long while before he would give judgment. Finally, so that all there might believe in his right to speak on this matter and not contest it afterwards, he told the story of how he had come by so great a store of wisdom concerning the Land and its division into comotes. Thus he told it, and thus was it told to me, in Ystrad Ffawr, while I undertook the long and arduous studies that befit a Bard for his office.

Once, Fintan said, there was another assembly of the men of Eriu, in the far-off time of Conaing Bececlach.[8] On one evening as the sun was setting, there came out of the west towards this assembly a wondrous figure. The height of a tree he was to the shoulder, and he had about him a kind of crystal veil. The sandals upon his feet were of no known material, and his hair streamed like a cloud of moving gold. In his left hand he held a tablet of stone, and in his right a silver branch on which were the fruits of three different trees—nut, apple, and acorn.

At first, all who were gathered there drew back in fear, but when they saw that the great being was about to stride past them with scarcely a glance in their direction, they called out to him.

And he, looking down from his height, said, "What do you desire of me?"

To which those assembled replied, "Who are you, and whither are you going?"

"My name," said he, "is Trefuilngid Treochair,[9] and I am going from the rising of the sun to the place of its setting."

"Why are you doing that?" they asked.

"Because it is I who causes the sun to rise and to set," was his reply.

At that there arose a murmur among the assembly, until one asked what had brought him to follow the sun, since it was his task anyway to bring it to its rest.

"Today," said the giant, "the sun stepped past me, and I set out to find what is amiss with it. For it failed to shine upon a part of the world in which a Jew was tortured and killed by the folk of Rome, and I would discover the cause."

Then the wise men of that assembly asked if Trefuilngid Treochair would return that way when he had discovered what he sought, for they, too, would know the answer. The giant promised that he would and strode on toward the place where the sun was even then setting.

The next day he returned as promised and told the assembly what he had learned of the death of one named Jesus. Though you may choose to doubt it, little monk, there were many there who wept to hear that tale and who vowed vengeance against the Romans for what they had done.

My master spoke directly here of a matter that has troubled me as much or more than it has troubled him—that we who follow the way of the Lord Christ are often intolerant of the ways of the wise ones from before the coming of the new way to the Island of the Mighty. Yet I marveled at the story he told, for whether it be truth or fable, it expressed rightly the nature of the pagan folk and their understanding of the wonders of the Lord Christ's life and teaching.

After this, the giant returned often to Eriu, showing that he was as eager as the men of that Land to remember the history of their race, which he claimed to have known long ages since, but lost sight of in carrying out his daily task. From his lips the men of Eriu learned much of their own early history, which was before that time lost to them. Fintan himself, then but a young man, learned much and remembered all, and this he now recited, over many days and nights, filling the minds and hearts of the assembly with wonder and delight.

Fintan told them that before Trefuilngid Treochair took leave of Eriu at last, he gave into their keeping one each of the fruits from the silver branch that he carried and instructed him in their use.[10] From these fruits the five Great Trees were planted that grew at the centers of the five comotes. The greatest of all was Eo Mugna, the Oak that grew in the center of Tara itself and cast a long shadow upon the earth. Its trunk was said to be thirty cubits around, and its height three hundred cubits. Its branches formed a canopy as broad as the plain upon which it grew, and its shade could offer shelter to a thousand warriors.

When Fintan had concluded his recital, he gave as his opinion the true division of the Land as it had been related to him by the ancient giant and as marked by the extent of the Great Trees themselves. This was a ruling none might contest without claiming greater wisdom. But there was none there who could do so, and thus the matter was settled among the people of Eriu for many ages after. As a poem written by one who was a Guardian of Eo Mugna says:

> *The acorn, the dark narrow nut,*
> *and the apple of joyful wisdom,*
> *were sent each year by the King*
> *as a blessing upon the Land.*

This state of affairs continued for many ages, until a dark time came upon Eriu. That time saw the fall of the Great Trees, which came about in this wise.

Many times there had been invasions into the sacred Land, such as are related in *The Book of Invasions*.[11] But at last there came a new kind of threat, and this, little monk, though it grieves me to say it, was the coming of the Brothers such as yourself who sought to sweep away all that had been and to replace it with new teachings. This I well understand to have been needful as they saw it, for to leave the signs and symbols of the old way active amid those of the new would seem to court disaffection and doubt. That folk cannot be left in peace to follow what belief they choose is ever a sign of the darkness that has overtaken humankind from the beginning, but such is, indeed, the way of things, and it is useless to inveigh against it.

In Eriu the conquest of the native folk by the followers of the new God was more gentle than in other lands. Many of your Brethren learned the ways of the old gods and gave them respect though others sought to destroy what had lasted for more ages than even the wisdom of the Cauldron and the Wood.

But it seems that when the poets who were then the Guardians of the Great Trees became aware that the people of Eriu were turning away from the old gods and looking towards the new, it came to them that they must take some action. Thus they came together, one day when the heavens themselves seemed to weep in sorrow for the changes that were come upon the Land, and they decided that the five Great Trees should be hidden from the sight of humankind.

And so it was done. But one Tree, Eo Rossa, which stood in Leinster, somehow became visible to the eyes of a monk named Molling, who in after time was called a saint by the followers of the new way. Perhaps, indeed, he was possessed of some special gift that enabled him to penetrate the Druid mist concealing the tree, but however it happened, he ordered the Tree felled so that he might use its timber to build a church.

You may believe that he found it hard to find anyone who would carry out this act, but in the end, he succeeded in finding a man named Gobban who, for a price, was willing to risk what might befall if axes were set to the sacred trunk of Eo Rossa. With the first stroke, a chip of wood flew into Molling's eye, so that he lost the sight of it from that time. But he was undeterred and ordered Gobban to continue. After two days of chopping, the Great Tree fell, doubtless to the accompaniment of many devout prayers. Such was its size, the fallen trunk covered many miles of Land, and its timbers, when cut, were sufficient to provide roofing for a dozen churches.

When the poets who were the Guardians of the four remaining trees heard what had happened, their anguish knew no bounds. Muirgen, who had been the Guardian of Eo Rossa, went alone into the mountains of Sleive na Ged and died there, whether from cold or from sorrow no one can say. As for the rest, Ninine, who was the Guardian of Eo Mugna and the senior of the four remaining poets, once again summoned his fellows to a meeting, and there they elected, with heavy hearts, to cut down the rest of the Great Trees themselves rather than risk their meeting the fate of Eo Rossa.

Now this plan was, as you may well understand, no easy task. Once the four poets had made their decision, which took many days of argument and discussion, they had next to find by what means the Trees were to be felled so that their sacredness would not be besmirched. For these were no ordinary trees. Grown from the fruits given to Fintan by Trefuilngid Treochair, they held much of the power of the Otherworld, as well as that of the High Kings of Eriu. At length, Ninine spoke out. "For this dread work, we require more strength than we together possess. Let us therefore summon every poet who remains in the Land, together with those in the Island of the Mighty, to come to our aid."

And so it was done. Never before and never since was such a gathering seen. Altogether seventy poets came together in a hidden place not far from where the shadow of Eo Munga fell. My own master, Talhearn, journeyed from Britain with twenty of the greatest poets ever to sit in the great choir of Ystrad Ffawr. More, every poet worthy of the name in all of Eriu came in answer to Ninine's summons, though there was not one who was not red-eyed with weeping at the thought of what they must do.

For nine days and nine nights they fasted, chanting the secret rhymes of their craft, until such power had been raised that even the greatest of the Great Trees might not withstand it. But in the end it is told that no axe blade was ever set to the holy wood, but that by the very power of their incantations, as well as the sorrow of their souls, Trefuilngid Treochair himself was summoned to be among them again. With the strength of the Otherworld and of the giver of the

Trees in his arm, he himself felled them, one by one, beginning with Eo Munga, until all four remaining Great Trees lay stretched upon the earth.

It is recorded that Eo Mugna fell southward and lay across more than half of its comote. Craeb Uisnig fell northward, Bile Tortan southeast, and Bile Dathi to the west, thus marking an ancient pattern in the earth that is still there—though hidden—to this day.[12] And it is further told, among the company of the wise, that although the Trees were seen to fall thus in the places and directions told, in another sense they did not fall, but were taken in their subtle essence back into the Otherworld from which they were sprung. Another telling that I have heard is that the Trees were cut up as had been Eo Rossa, and that branches were taken and planted in the earth, and that from them grew a particularly deep and powerful part of the Wood. But whether that be true or not, even I cannot tell. All that I will say is that in my time at Ystrad Ffawr, I learned an ancient poem about Eo Mugna, which saluted the Great Tree in this wise:

> *Tree of Mugna:*
> *King's Wheel,*
> *Prince's right,*
> *Wave's thunder,*
> *Finest creature,*
> *Firm, straight tree.*
> *Banba's truth,*
> *Power of victory,*
> *Origin's judge,*
> *Scion of sages,*
> *Noblest tree,*
> *Glory of Tara,*
> *Life's vigor,*
> *Knowledge spell—*
> *Tree of Mugna!*[13]

The felling of the Great Trees—or their removal to the Otherworld, which-ever tale you choose to believe—marked the end of the old ways in Eriu. Yet it was not the end truly, but a beginning, for there were those of both the old and the new faiths who could speak to each other and who, being learned in the lore of each kind, drew upon both for the food of the spirit. One such, a woman named Brigid after the goddess of song and who had studied long in the colleges of the old ways, by chance and circumstance came to be taken in by holy women of the new faith. Such was her wisdom and brightness of spirit that she rose to be abbess of her order and spread the word of both faiths far and wide. Once, it is said, she came to Glaston itself, where the holy relic of your God's Passion later resided, as I have told elsewhere.[14]

But never again did the Great Trees flourish in Eriu, and I fear that unless there are great changes in the Land, much the same fate will in time be meted out to those Great Trees that still grow, though hidden, in the Island of the Mighty, with what effect may be judged by the later fate of Eriu.

Of all that my master told me, this story has disturbed me most deeply. If he spoke the truth here, as I believe him to have done from the start, then these Trees still stand, and must indeed be permitted to remain untouched, for the good of the Land which I too, as did he, love deeply. And I perceive that, whether or not I might accept their import, his words may not be ignored. I have prayed long on this matter and have found that I must preserve this story along with the rest, despite what its meaning may be for those who follow the way of the Lord Christ. For I must believe, with my master, that all truths are ultimately one truth, and this I have indeed come to recognize, even though it cost me my soul.

THE SILENCE OF WINTER

Silence crawled across the snowfields.
It lapped against the walls of the castle.
Pale wintry sunlight flashed silver
From the branches of trees
And the frozen stems of grass
That rattled together like naked finger joints.

I stood on the snow-lipped parapet,
Stared towards hills where something gleamed.
Behind me, on the castle's further side,
A black river ran, from which arose
Cold coils of mist, so that the water
Seemed to smoke, breathing on the sharp air.
Waiting, I listened to the silence,
Felt it approach along the ground like a drowning wave.
Only where I stood was there life.
My face seemed dead,
Yet my lips moved and my eyes saw . . .
                              Then,
My fingers flew, flashed white
On the gray walls, and from my lips,
Words poured . . .
    In answer to my summons
The light that moved across the waste
Warmed and grew golden suddenly.
Out of the still and golden sky
Birdsong fell. Beyond my sight a bird flew,
Let fall a feather that floated to rest
At my feet . . .

At length I looked down,
Fell silent and grew still again.
Slowly the silence drew back.
The black waters of the river received it.
And with a sound like indrawn breath,
Sounds of nearing Spring returned.
On the far hills the silver quivered.
A single speck flashed momentary gold.

15
THE HUNTING OF HEN WEN

reat wisdom and great teaching are never easy to find, nor is the means of their transmission always simple to trace. In all my days in the Wood, and before that at Ystrad Ffawr, I heard many strange stories that bore within them the fruits of ancient teaching. Since then, I myself have oftentimes used the method of concealing truth within tales, and much that I have told you before this day, and will tell you after it, is meant to be understood in this way. ❧ The story I shall tell you now is based on events through which I lived and the outcome of which I saw and heard, either with my physical eyes or through the windows of the Wood. Yet you must understand that not all my words are meant to be like glass through which one may see clearly. As Merlin said once: my words shall be as darkness to some; as mirrors to others.

This was the only time my master ever spoke at all directly of the method of teaching which, I now believe, qualifies much of what he told me. Certainly, of all the stories I wrote down at his bidding, this one seems to me most strange.

This is a tale about Cai, who was Arthur's foster brother in the House of Antor. I have heard people speak of Cai the Braggart, Cai the Coward, Cai of the Cutting Tongue,[1] and to be sure there was that about Arthur's steward that was neither lovely nor likeable. But, as this story shows, once, at least, he performed a great feat, one that deserves to be remembered and which needs to be told, not merely for the part he played in it, but also because it brings together two more strains of the tale of Arthur in the wards of Broceliande.

I have already spoken of the Great Sow Hen Wen,[2] which the warband of Arthur encountered when they went forth to help the High King's nephew Culhwch in his quest for Olwen. And I spoke then of the prophecy that told how one day the Old White One would bring destruction to the Island of the Mighty. For Hen Wen was an offspring of one of the seven magical pigs that were brought out of Annwn, and it was said that one day she would give birth to an offspring that would cause such trouble for the people of the Island that it would be spoken of for many ages to come.

For a long time Arthur brooded upon this prophecy, until finally he could not rest until he had destroyed the Great Sow. So, he gathered his warband and set out for the pig runs of Pendaren Dyfedd. Now that strange man knew of Arthur's approach almost before the Ymerawdwr had set foot in the stirrup, and when Arthur and his men arrived before his gate, they found Pendaren standing before it, forbidding them admittance.

"I know why you have come, Arthur of Britain," said he. "But you shall not enter this place unless you first defeat me."

"I have no quarrel with you, Pendaren Dyfedd," said Arthur. "But I will see the blood of Hen Wen spilled upon the earth this day."

But Pendaren stood unmoved. "I say that you shall not pass unless you sustain three falls against me at wrestling."

Hand upon his sword, Arthur considered. Then with a laugh he took off his splendid helm with the crest of the snarling boar, laid aside his great sword, took off his coat of finest mail, and stood in his shirt facing the powerful swineherd.

Then such a match began as never has been seen before or since in the Island of the Mighty. The two men fought like bears or wolves, and neither could get any advantage of the other. Then Pendaren threw the Ymerawdwr to the earth and pinned him there. He rose, and again they fought; but this time it was Arthur who, by sheer strength, bore his opponent to the earth. A final time they fought, and for a long time again neither had the advantage, until perhaps by some skill half-remembered from his childhood in the Wood, Arthur broke his opponent's hold and threw him so heavily to the earth that Pendaren lay unmoving for several minutes.

Then Arthur put on again his mail coat and helm, took up his sword and shield, and went forth towards the pig run. At that, there was a terrible crashing and rending and squealing, and from within the enclosure burst the great White Sow herself, her red ears flapping, her vast body quivering. The warband scattered before her like so much chaff, and then she was gone, leaving a trampled wake of undergrowth behind her.

At once the warband gave chase, letting loose the dogs to pursue the quarry. But Hen Wen was no ordinary beast. Her lineage was of the Otherworld and her power like no other creature in all the Island of the Mighty, except perhaps for the mighty Trwch Trwth, who was hunted by Arthur on another occasion.[3]

So began the strangest chase of any that is recorded in this Land. For try as they might, the warband could not catch up with the Old White One. They would have needed magic to do so. This they could have had, but Arthur gave out that this task must be accomplished by human bone and sinew and blood.

Thus the hunt continued, throughout all that day, until the Old White One came to the shore of the sea at Penrhyn Awstein in Cornwall. There she entered the water of the narrow sea[4] and swam across to the farther shore. And there, in the wheat fields of Gwent, she paused long enough to give birth. It is told that she dropped a strange litter—a grain of wheat and a bee—and that from that time, the Land of Gwent has been famed for its plentiful wheat and its rich honey. But this is but to say that Hen Wen left behind her the symbols of her Otherworldly power, for as all who have drunk of the Cauldron know, these two things are signs of transformation and rebirth—old secrets, little monk, which must remain secrets for the present time, but which will one day be revealed.[5]

Then Hen Wen set forth again, running as fast as the wind and as tirelessly, while the warband with Arthur at its head trailed behind her. She entered the cantref of Pembroke and there gave birth to a grain of barley and a grain of wheat, also symbols of regeneration such as were once common in the Land. But still the warband could not catch her, and the Great Sow ran still further into Arfon, until she reached the Hill of Cyferthwch. There she gave birth to a wolf cub and an eagle, and it is said that these two were given to Mergaed and Breat, two princes of that Land, but that no good came from this gift.[6]

At last, at Llanfair in Arfon, under a great stone called the Black Rock, Hen Wen turned at bay, and there the warband caught up with her and slew her, so that her blood darkened the earth. It is said that because of this slaughter, the people of the Otherworld ever after bore ill will towards Arthur and sent many of their kind to trouble him. This I believe to be so, for how else can so much that happened in his time be explained?[7]

But this is not the end of the story. For when the dogs had done their bloody work, the body of Hen Wen's last offspring was found breathing amidst the carnage. This offspring was a black kitten of no more than two hands' span. Cai, who rode with the warband that day, took the creature and flung it into the sea, from which act he was destined to earn both great trouble and great fame, as you shall see.

This was the way of it.

The sea carried the last offspring of Hen Wen to the shores of Môn. There it was washed ashore, half drowned, and taken in by the sons of Palug, half-wild children of the Sea People, who were said to walk on two legs on the land but to grow tails when they swam in the sea. There the Cat grew rapidly into a great beast, half as big as the great hall at Kidwelly. It became known as Cath Palug, the Cat of the Palugs.[8] There, too, it was found by Pendaren Dyfedd, who had set out

166

to follow the hunt when he recovered from the mighty throw given him by Arthur. Between the swineherd and the Great Cat grew an understanding such as he once had with Hen Wen herself. Soon, the beast began marauding inland across the island of Môn, spreading further afield, until it began hunting in the lands of Pembroke and of Gwynedd, killing and destroying everything it came upon.

At length word of this ravaging reached the ears of the Ymerawdwr himself, and he began at once to prepare a warband against the Cat. But Cai heard of it first and slipped away by himself. "For," he said, "it was my task to kill the last of Hen Wen's spawn, and it is my failure to do so that has brought this trouble upon us. Therefore I shall go myself to see to it." And forth he went, on the swiftest horse, arriving on the shore of Pembroke, from which the cliffs of Môn could clearly be seen, far in advance of the rest of the warband. There he settled to wait the coming of Cath Palug, sharpening his sword the while in readiness.

After a time he heard a great commotion; and peering around the rock behind which he had taken station, he saw the Great Cat attack and kill a deer within a bowshot of his hiding place. It was indeed a huge and terrible beast, and his blood turned chill as he looked at it. But for all his deep dislike of his fellow men, Cai was no coward, and tightening his grip on his sword, he climbed onto the rock that had given him shelter and, screaming his battle cry, flung himself onto the back of Cath Palug.

With a wailing screech the Cat leapt high in the air, landing with bone jarring force on all four feet. Cai was almost thrown off, but he dug his fingers deep into the Cat's thick fur and stabbed it in the neck again and again. Howling and screeching, Cath Palug staggered and shook, twisting its huge head around in an attempt to bite the warrior from its back. But Cai clung on like a wasp and kept hacking with his sword until his arm seemed like to drop off and his breath came and went like fire in his lungs.

At length, after what seemed an age of hacking and stabbing, the Great Cat fell dying, its blood pouring out onto the earth. Cai, weak and trembling like a day-old cub, fell off and lay half-dead for hours. When he roused, the Cath Palug lay stiffening at his side. He cut off one of its great front feet and left the rest where it lay, to the delight of circling carrion.

Thus Cai achieved his one truly great deed, one that earned him the praise of all the warband. And thus fell the last offspring of Hen Wen. A song, composed by Aneurin, remembers it still:

> *Cai the fair went to Môn,*
> *To destroy the last of Hen Wen's brood.*
> *His shield was a bastion*
> *Against Palug's Cat.*
> *When it is asked,*
> *Who killed the great beast,*
> *Nine score champions utter*
> *The name of fair Cai.*[9]

TALIESIN AND THE ALTERNATIVES

As the Three Drops fell on his finger, Taliesin sang:
"Gwion no longer, all time runs in me now, like a river,
Downward to a sea that carries in its sunless womb
The tides of all men's striving for the truth,
Setting a seal on all our lifelong ills
And leaving us no alternatives but death or birth.

16

THE DEFENSE OF THE CHAIR

here are stories in every life that are less cause for pride than others. Such a one is that which I must tell now, for such things should not be left in the dark too long, lest they grow crooked and out of shape. ❧ "Perfect is my Chair in Caer Siddi." How often have I sung those words, written after I first went into Annwn,[1] concerning my own connection with that Otherworldly realm that gave birth to the Cauldron and, maybe, to the Wood itself, and from which so much of my knowledge springs. Yet there is another Chair, of which I have not spoken before, to which I must return periodically and which is mine by right until another comes to take my place.

I believe these words to have been written only shortly before my master left me for good. Yet from the mention in the story of Owein, son of Urien, the events referred to must have taken place long before, in the early days of the Ymerawdwr Arthur, before my master came to serve him as Royal Poet. Thus it took him many years to speak of the things of

which he writes here. There remains much that is strange and fearful about this tale, much that I cannot understand. Yet, even as I write these words, there is a part of me that does understand. It is a part that I have long kept hidden within me, lest I be thought false in my beliefs. Yet it is there nonetheless, and perhaps it is this neglected side of my nature that drew me to my Lord Taliesin in the first place, though I cannot be certain of this.

After the Battle of Goddeu Brig and the voyage of Bran to Ireland to reave back the Cauldron of Annwn, there grew to be a great animosity between Arawn, Lord of the Underworld, and myself. He knew the part I had played in the Battle of the Trees and, even more surely, he knew of my dedication to the Wood, which, in some part, contains us all. Thus he laid a trap for me, one he knew I could neither avoid nor refuse. It was a trap suited to a poet, who cannot ever cease from inquiry and whose life is one with the Land.

It began one night when I was in the royal Dun (stronghold) of Owein, son of Urien, whom I served at that time in the office of poet. There I dreamed that a man with a cold, harsh face stood before me. He seemed at once both familiar and strange, though I could not have said why. He said, "The Chair of Prydein stands empty. Why do you not take your rightful place within it?"

Even in my vision my heart grew cold when I heard these words. To understand why this should be, I must give some account of the Chair of which the stranger spoke, for in our time, the knowledge of such things is at best despised, if not utterly forgotten. The chair is no less than the hereditary seat of the inner Guardians of the Island of the Mighty. Each Land, little monk, has an inner place of spiritual truth from which all that is best and most perfect to it emerges. In that place sits one who is both Guardian and seer and who watches over the fate of the lands above.

The Chair of Prydein is thus a chair both in name and in fact, but so deeply hidden that none may find it unless they are bidden there. Only one may sit there at any time, and whoever does so must be the strongest in will, the most subtle in mind, and the most deeply versed in the wisdom of the Otherworld, since it is this one's task to gather the strands of life in the Lands Above and bring them together in the Lands Beneath.

Even I did not know the names of those who had sat in the Chair before the time of which I speak, only that they were all singers of great power who had drunk deeply of the Cauldron's wisdom. Nor had I known until that moment that the Chair stood empty, though afterwards I understood that much of what passed in that time—war and strife and a terrible, insatiable hunger that gripped the Island of the Mighty—was because of this.

Thus, to hear myself invited to take my place in the Chair brought with it both fear and wonder, for this was a great thing, indeed, for anyone who served the Land. The wonder I felt came from a sense of challenge, for I knew that it would be no easy thing to win the Chair and that I would be tested to the limits of my knowledge. Fear I knew also, for this was no light matter to undertake, but rather a great and terrible burden. Since that time, I have often wondered what my life would have been had I refused this test. But it seemed to me then something I could not refuse, something for which I had been preparing from the moment I drank Ceridwen's brew.

So, with the brash confidence of one but lately come into his true power, I looked into the face of the stranger and asked, "How may I come there?" For the way was hidden, even to me, at that time.

But he merely shook his head and smiled, though there was no mirth in his look. "That you must discover for yourself, if you dare."

I awoke, sweating, knowing that this was no dream, but a true sending, which I might not ignore.

So, because I had drunk of the Cauldron and because I was a Son of the Wood, I set out that very morning to find my way to the place of the Chair. Long I journeyed, and many strange and terrible things I saw, for I went by no ordinary route, but took instead the paths that lead between the worlds, where all appearances are deceptive, though in fact they are real in a way that the shadow world in which we live can never be. For in such places one may see only true reality, where patterns are fashioned from which all the worlds are shaped.[2]

Thus I went, by the high and narrow track that winds always between the Hollow Hills of the Sidhe, until I came at last to the edge of a tideless sea where a boat without sail or rudder awaited me. No sooner had I stepped within than it began to move, carrying me swiftly to the place I sought.

Soon I saw where an island rose from the sea, and as I drew nearer, I saw that it was surrounded by three circles of fire that burned in the midst of the water in defiance of all natural laws.

At first I knew fear. Then I remembered something I had learned from a Master of the Secret Fire, and drawing my harp from where it rode, as ever, at my back, I played notes that outran the flames themselves, so that they parted before me and I sailed through to the shore of the isle.

It was a small enough place, with but a single tower built upon it, tall and grim and seeming empty. Before it stood an ornate fountain, shaped like a great stone vessel, carved with intricate patterns about the rim. There water rose and fell and sparkled like jewels in the air. Suddenly I knew a great and abiding thirst, though I knew also and with as great a certainty that I must not drink. To do so would be to wipe out all I had learned, to drown my thoughts in a forgetfulness from which I would never wake. And so I passed the fountain by and entered the tower.

I found myself within a single chamber, rising all the way to the top of the tower, through which I could see hurrying clouds. There, in the center, was the Chair of Prydein, a simple stone seat with a high back and rests for the arms. As I approached it, a figure stood before me who had not been there a moment before. It was Arawn himself, his face showing only triumph. It was then that I knew, past uncertainty, a truth that pride and eagerness had hidden from me. My coming there had been, from the start and however arranged, a plot on the part of the Lord of Annwn.

"So, poet, you have come, as I knew you would. Your pride was too great to refuse such an offer."

I knew that what he said was all too true, but I summoned what protection I might to cover me from his regard and answered, as lightly as I might, "I am here, as you see. But since when has the Chair of Prydein been in the gift of Annwn's Lordship?"

Arawn's face darkened still further, and I saw that, beyond expectation, I had struck a blow against my enemy. It was only then, for the first time, that I began to suspect that we were both pawns, he and I, in some greater game.

"Anyone foolish enough to believe himself fitted for this office must soon discover how little he knows," said Arawn. But I knew that he could not answer my question directly, for to do so would have been to admit that he was there by another's connivance.

"Such is well known," I said, "but I will try nonetheless." I said these words with less confidence than I showed, though Arawn must have known my mind. But he stood aside, allowing me access to the Chair. And I saw then, without surprise, that another sat in it—a shadowy figure, so draped about that it was impossible to tell whether it was man or woman. Then came a voice, which I heard not in words but inside my head.

"Who demands the right to sit in the Chair of Prydein?"

I gave my name and titles.

"Do you know what is entailed for the one who sits where I now sit?"

"I do."

"Then answer me these questions."

So began an exchange of riddles, the form of which had been laid down from a time before Time. Only the wisdom of the Cauldron sustained me, enabling me to answer as I did.

The first question: "From where have you come?"

I answered without hesitation. "From known lands, and unknown lands, that I may discover the place where knowledge and ignorance are born, the place where they died, and the place where they are buried."

And the second: "What is the sea that was about us formally?"

Again, I answered with the required words. "It was flowery; it was green; it was hilly; it was filled with rivers and streams. It was rich in silver; it was filled with chariots. When I was a hound, I abandoned it; when I was a salmon, and a bird, and a hare, I took up my abode here. Though I knew neither father nor mother, yet I have drunk of the Mother's brew and have dwelled in the Wood."

And the third: "What lies to the west of here?"

"Islands."

"And what is beneath them?"

"Longhaired men who sing with wondrous voices; terrible kine whose lowing is tuneful; herds of deer; unknown lands with green hills above the churning water."

In this fashion, the questioning continued, though I may not speak of it here at more length. But it seemed that I gave the correct answers to every question that was asked, for at the last, the shadowy figure arose from the Chair and bade me take my place there.

But this I knew to be yet another test, and so I replied that I would not until the speaker revealed herself. For during the long colloquy, I had had the chance to study my interlocutor and believed that I knew who it was that I faced.

The figure grew taller, threw off the muffling cloak, and I saw one stand before me whose brightness was as a dazzling light to me, so that I bowed my head. Then I felt placed in my hands a cup. I looked within it, and it was filled with clear water. Then the voice of my questioner said, speaking clearly now: "This is the four-sided Cup of Truth, which I gave to Cormac long since.[3] Drink now, and receive your just honor."

So I drank, and what I learned then I may not speak of or write even now, though I have told most other things. It is, as I have said, not out of fear that I keep silence, but from an inability to express the inexpressible. Even I, Taliesin, admit this. It is also true that there are some things it is neither right nor meet for men to know, for the knowledge brings with it a hard responsibility that must first be won.

ven now, as I read these words, I feel a shiver of fear. I know that my master had access to many mysteries that will seem unwholesome to those who, like my self, honor the Lord Christ. Yet, as I have written before, I do not believe them to be innately evil. Nor may I forget the stillness and look of deep joy that came over my master whenever he spoke of these things.

When I had drunk of the Cup of Truth, I took my place in the Chair of Prydein, as others had done before me, unto the very beginning of time. And she, holding her hands above me, laid upon me the blessing and the curse of my office, that I must guard and guide the Land and all who had charge of it. It was revealed to me then, as I had long suspected, that the last to sit there had been Merlin himself, and that he had departed now beyond the reach of any man, though whether to a madman's cave or the realm of the Ever-Living I cannot say. What I do know, assuredly, is that his fate was not slavery to the maiden of the Lake Nimue.

Since I was now to take his place, my first task must be to guide the foot-steps of the Ymerawdwr Arthur. For though he had long since established his kingdom after the fashion of men and had set up the great Fellowship of the Round Table, he had still to walk the path of that great quest, which was to absorb both him and his Company for so many long, hard years.[4]

It was then, too, that I began to perceive the first glimmering of other knowl-edge: of Arthur, of his Queen Gwenhwyfar, and of the true nature of the quest itself, which was not only for the cup of Christ, but also for the Cauldron.

In all that time I had been unaware of what passed in the chamber, but when I looked about me now, I found that I was alone. My eyes were drawn to the sky above the tower, and I saw that it was night. How long I had sat in the Chair of Prydein I could not say. Slowly, then, the truth was born upon me. The trap that had been set for me by the Lord of Annwn, which had been meant to bring me low before the Goddess of the Land, was the means by which I might take up this office, one which I may not lay down, even now. For though I have walked far within this world that so many know as the only truth, and have watched both the wonders and terrors of the High King's reign, the Chair awaits me still, and calls to me, as it will continue to do until another is sent to take my place.

erhaps it is not foolish to believe that, in the end, another did come who would bear the burden of which my master spoke. For how else may I understand his passing from this world—whether to the death he came, I believe, to desire, or to that Otherland of which he spoke so eloquently and that even I, who might not listen, sometimes half-longed to see? If I understand his words even a little, no other means could be found to release him from the burden of his office.

THE MYSTERIES OF SEVEN

I am Taliesin,
Divine Child of the Mother.
I speak in riddles
From the Fountain of Vision.
My words are for those
Who understand
The roots of trees,
The secrets of earth.
Let me tell how the sun
Gilded the Hero's face;
Receive from me the secret
Of my Mother's seven names.
Three times seven and then three
Were the number of her priestesses;
Two times seven and then two
Were the number of her poets.
Twelve shadows she had
And six faces;
Nine were the maidens
Who breathed above her Cauldron
To prevent it from boiling.
Five were the number
Of her skirts in heaven,
Only the god
Might raise them all.
Four kept watch
At the Tower of the Winds.
Two were her progeny
Except for myself.

But I am first,
The last of the poets
To sing her praise:
My tongue silvered,
My brow radiant,
My throat pure,
My dreams of her.

17

THE PROTECTION OF
THE HONEY ISLE

s I have told you, little monk, every Land has an Inner Land, a secret heart whose beat is strong or weak according to the Land's health. That health is dependent upon the health of the King, the ruler who makes his bargain with Lady Sovereignty[1] and keeps it as best he might. Of Arthur, and how he made his bargain with the Lady, and of the whole strange, dark matter of those times, I have spoken all that I may. But there is another tale to tell, one which touches me more directly, and which has not been told. Since it is part of the greater tales of the Wood, I shall tell it here for those with the wit to understand its meaning. ✒ The Inner Land of the Island of the Mighty— the Honey Isle, or Clas Myrddyn, or Logres, to mention but a few of the island's secret names—exists as part of the Land as it is seen by all men, but yet possesses another dimension, a shadow-self that lies within and behind the surface of the world. Here the ancient wise ones, of whom Merlin was one, and the Old One herself, and the Lady of the Lake another, have their being and maybe their origin too, though that is less certain. Here they dwell, and so long as they are there, there can be no ending to that inner place.[2]

Yet from time to time there have arisen those who would contest the power of the wise, or who sought to control their power, little knowing that this power could be no more harnessed than the very elements themselves. One such who sought this power was the sorceress Anowre. She had the blood of the Sidhe-folk in her veins, and a deal of knowledge besides, much of it gained through no natural means. Yet still she was hungry for more—for the power that would enable her to control others.

Several times she attempted to gain power over Arthur himself. Once she kidnapped him and offered herself as a bedfellow. But when he awoke from the false sleep she had laid upon him and found her in bed at his side, he turned away from her coldly, and no word or blandishment she could offer would suffice to make him even so much as look at her.

At that she rose and commanded Arthur to follow her to the heights of the tower where she dwelled. There she showed him the wide and beautiful lands upon every side and swore that she would turn them to dust and ashes if he would not bed with her. But still Arthur refused, and for his pains spent many more weeks in prison, until Nimue, who had proved an apt pupil of Merlin's, set him free.

I recall other occasions when my master spoke of a succession of "Guardians" who had the keeping of the kingdom in their care. These he described as the holders of the Chair of Prydein. He himself was one such, as he has told in the tale here titled "The Defense of the Chair." It seems that Nimue—she of whom such dark stories are told, such as that she imprisoned Merlin beneath a rock, which my master holds to be a lie—was another.

But Anowre did not stop when this scheme was foiled, and some time after, she succeeded in stealing Arthur's sword Excalibur, the great blade of the

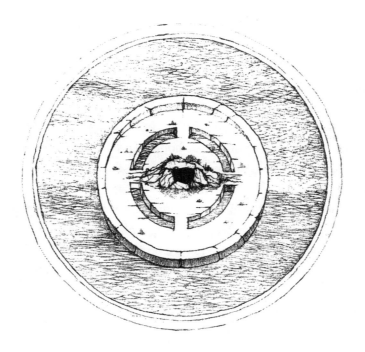

PROTECTION OF THE HONEY ISLE

Pendragons without which none might truly rule in the Island of the Mighty. How she achieved this feat was learned only after the events I am about to relate: how she cast a cloak of invisibility about herself and entering the palace, found her way to Arthur's own chamber, and seized the sword. Why the blade did not cry out in her grasp is uncertain. Perhaps her Faery blood was sufficient to make it seem that a fit hand was grasping it.

Later, the story was twisted to tell how it was the King's half-sister Morgain who took the sword, and that while it was in her possession, the scabbard that protected the King from all hurt was lost. How such a tale ever came to be told of one who had as much right as Arthur to hold the sword is but further evidence of the misshaping of the truth that began at the moment when the King departed for Avalon. The true story shall now be told. I shall hold back nothing, even though it reflects badly upon myself.

Word of the theft reached me quickly, for such a thing sends tremors through the very fabric of the Wood. The king's sword was stolen; the king was thereby in danger, and thus the Land itself at peril. The strength of the Pendragon blood, so long prepared and bred to this great moment in time, was weakened by this loss, for its deepest and innermost power was bound up within the blade, upon which were written runes that none might read save those who held the sword in trust for the wise.

I knew where I should find Anowre, in her tower in that part of the Wood known as the Perilous Forest. A dark enough place it was, and one I had no desire to visit. Yet go I must, if I were to recover the sword. Two days later, I stood before the door of the tower and called upon the sorceress to give up that which was not hers.

Truthfully I had not expected her to deny me, but this she did, flinging her mockery from a window above me. I at once drew forth my harp and played a series of chords that should have opened any door. Yet the entrance to Anowre's tower remained firmly shut. Then, for the first time, I began to feel fear. By my reckoning there should have been no way that Anowre could wield the sword, and her own magic was as nothing beside that of those who had brought the ancient weapon to birth. That she had succeeded in taking the weapon and now had the strength to hold it against me meant that there must be another factor in the puzzle of which I was unaware.

I retired into the shelter of the forest to meditate upon the matter further, sitting, knees drawn up to chin, hands clasped around them, eyes closed, amid the trees. I went deeply inward, almost as deeply as I knew how, before I found what I sought. An image came to me. It was of a desolate place, a nearly dry lake between high cliffs. Rising from the center was a low, wide-topped mound, into which had been dug moats filled with water. In the center, as though it had been transplanted there from some other place, an area of rough, broken ground lay exposed. Giant stones framed the entrance to a cavern, from the mouth of which drifted a plume of smoke.

I stared at this image for some time, trying to fathom what I was seeing. This was no place that I knew, in any of the worlds, yet it seemed strangely familiar to me, as though I had been there long since, so long ago that I had forgotten it. Then, as I watched—and I was surely watching a real event rather than a dream produced by my own art—I saw movement within the cave mouth. It was as though something vast was dragging itself, inch by sluggish inch, towards the entrance to its lair.

With that thought came a realization, a cold blast of fear that drove me back into my body. I half fell, lying twisted upon one side, my heart hammering. I was remembering an image that had haunted me ever since I had first encountered it, long since, in Merlin's Tower, when we had studied the creation of the Worlds together and witnessed the coming of a great serpent creature. This creature, I knew, was the nemesis that threatened Arthur and all that the Land stood for. It was a beast beyond our power to measure, beyond our wills to contain. I doubted that even the combined strength of the Ancients could turn it aside. It was a specter more terrible than any I had ever witnessed, more terrible even than the pictures I had been vouchsafed long ago in the cave of Ceridwen.

his beast to which my master refers may well be likened to that which is described in the writings of the blessed St. John, which I remember from my days in the little monastery among the hills. That such a creature could have threatened us in my own lifetime is a thought that brings only terror in its wake.

In a while, I sat up, calmed my thudding heart, took out my harp and began to play, softly. Thus was I able to think. Somehow, Anowre had made a link with the serpent beast. It was this link that gave her the strength to wield Excalibur, which had been created from the blood of serpents in the smithy beneath the Lake.[3] With that thought I knew that I must go to the Lady of the Lake herself, though there was small love lost between us. True, we shared more than a bloodline, but in her fashioning of Ancelot, she had sown seeds that could bear only barren fruit.

As I understand my master in the many talks we had together concerning these things, it was already known what would come of the love between Arthur's Queen and his foremost knight. Yet because of the pattern laid down by the Mighty Ones whom the Lord Taliesin served, these things could not be changed. Even these Mighty Ones served yet greater Lords—the equivalent, mayhap, of the Angelic Ones who go at all times between Heaven and Earth, carrying messages to and from the Throne of the Most High.

Thus I found myself again entering the strange, twilight world of the Lady, where I had sworn long since never to go again. Beneath the Lake all is mysterious and undefined, and to walk there is to walk as in a dream that has neither beginning nor end. It took all the strength of my mind to keep the images of the world above, of the Land and the Wood, from growing blurred and opaque. Yet I did so, and at last I stood before the Lady, who smiled slowly at me and hooded her gaze.

"I know why you are here, my poet. What would you have me do?"

"You are the Guardian of the Sword. You understand its power better than any. Can you not command it against Anowre?"

"You forget that I am no longer the Sword's Guardian. That task is Arthur's for as long as he is King."

"Yet still you have command over it."

"I am not its maker; therefore my command over it is small."

"Then what of Anowre?"

"It is not Anowre that you have to fear. Surely you knew that, or you would not have come here." She smiled lazily. "It is the Dragon you must overcome."

"You know that is beyond the power of us all, even if we were all brought together."

"But there is another, whom you have forgotten. One who is neither part of the Land nor separate from it."

Into my mind there came at these words the image of a face. It was one I had not thought of for many years, but which had yet never been far from my mind.

Touched with unearthly beauty, it was the face of the child god, Mabon, son of Modron. Long since I had helped release him from the prison of Echymeint, where he had been bound by an ancient enemy. Because of this I believed I might call upon Mabon to aid me in this time of greatest need. For, as the Lady had said, he stood outside the pattern of the Land's destiny and could therefore act when no other might.[4]

T his Mabon of whom my master speaks is known as a god of youth among the older races of the Island of the Mighty, where he is called simply Son, son of Mother. Often have I wondered, on hearing of him, if he might not be an echo of the Lord Christ, who was also a Son of the Mother, but of such things it is perilous to speak in this time. Nor, though I have looked often, have I found the tale of how my master helped free him. Yet clearly there was a debt that was owed and upon which my master now called, at what price he speaks hereafter.

Remembering those events long past, it was indeed as though a part of my mind that had long been closed suddenly opened, and from the chamber within came sunlight. I looked at the Lady and gave her my heartfelt thanks.

Gently mocking seemed her reply to me. "Farewell, Taliesin, until we next meet."

All too soon I was to understand that her look contained sorrow and pity also, but then I was too eager to depart for the place from which I might call out to the god.

Leaving the halls of the Land Beneath the Lake, I made haste to the ancient stone that bears his name and that was once an altar stone in time so distant that even my knowledge of it is slight. There I made offering and played an old song that I had all but forgotten.

> *I am a child of rowan and I bring you berries.*
> *From the West I come*

and my smile is the smile
of one you knew long since.
Through you is the blessing
of light and the green world
made open to all;
and in the sunset I am born
that say unto you:
I am a child of rowan—
I am barley.

There, quietly, the young god came and stood at my side, shading his eyes with one hand to look out across the Land. From the Mabanstane,[5] one may see much of the Island of the Mighty, and on this day it looked as fair as it had ever looked, so that my heart rose in my breast and threatened to choke me.

The slim, bright figure of the god stood silent for a long time, looking. Then he said, "What you ask is no easy thing. Nor is the price a small one. I can turn aside the beast from its course, send it back deep into its lair. But only for a time, for it must come forth one day, as is its right. Are you willing to pay the price that will be demanded if I do this thing?"

What could I have said? Even had I known the meaning of the god's words, could I have answered otherwise? My fate and the life of the Land were entwined in every way, and there was no life of any other kind that I could contemplate. I nodded my ascent.

The young god lifted his hand in a curiously tender gesture, as though pushing something from him: "Then so be it. I can do no more, for the pattern must take its course, as must all things. Farewell."

He was gone as suddenly as he had come, and I felt a moment of loss that broke through the walls I had long since erected about myself against such feelings. But this was not a time for dreams, for I still had work to do.

Going by paths known only to those who are at one with the Wood, I returned to Anowre's tower. This time the door opened at my command, and I entered. But the tower was dead and had the look of a place long abandoned. I left there and returned to Camelot with all speed. There I found that at the moment when I had stood in the presence of the god, Anowre herself had entered the hall where the King sat and gave back Excalibur into his hands. Men said that her look spoke of terror and that she walked as one in a dream. She departed and was seen no more in the Island of the Mighty.

I alone guessed the price, which must have been extracted from her in return for the power to take the sword and hold it against me. For those who make alliance with the Dragon do so at their peril, and no less than the gift of her own life could have been enough to give Anowre the strength I had felt within her.

Foolishly, I believed this to be the price the god had named. Later I was to learn otherwise, to my cost, and to understand the look of sorrow in the eyes of the Lady. Now, long after these events, I believe that nothing less than the death of Arthur's only son—slain, it seemed, without reason—was the price the god demanded for turning back the Dragon. That loss, which helped unbalance the kingdom and deprived the Land of one who might otherwise have achieved the quest for the Cauldron, stuck more deeply into the heart of Logres —and into my own heart also—than almost any other event in the history of the Ymerawdwr.

It is easy enough to look back upon such events and to believe that had I not gone to the Lady, or sought the help of the god, none of what followed would have taken place. Yet in my heart, I do not believe this, for my life in the wards of the Wood has taught me how certain patterns are laid down from the start and may not be altered. Thus the death of Llacheu has a purpose, even though our sorrow blinded us to it.

Nor would the beast be turned aside for long, for as Mabon had told me, it would have its day. When Anowre's theft of the sword was all but forgotten, the Dragon would return, stronger than ever, and this time only the death of the High King himself would appease it.

Thus a pattern would be repeated, which had been present since the first days, a pattern in which a chosen one would come and blaze a bright track across the heavens, until the time came to encounter the beast. Again and again this encounter would take place, and again and again, the one who took up the challenge would return to the Lands Beneath.

That Arthur was such a one is only half-understood in this time and may soon be forgotten altogether. For this reason I have spoken of these things, in the hope that they may be remembered. Only thus may those who follow learn how shaky is the balance of the world upon the edge of the abyss, and how easily it may be dislodged.

Again, these words fill me with fear, for if my master spoke the truth, and I have no honest reason to doubt him, then we are in mortal danger still, unless the King returns.

TALIESIN AND THE DARK

I was born before the dark
and seeing its conception,
understanding its nature,
am myself part of it.

My acts are acts of contrition.

I walk naked in the dark,
body blazing with true fire;
my hands weaving subtle strains of power,
my sight shining blue as broken sky.

Love and hate bide together in my thought.

I understand the unicorn's song,
and my own is made of owls and flowers;
I have made my voice of night and time;
my shadow goes before me like a spear.

Yet at sunrise night bows low.

18

THE DEATH OF ANEURIN

It is very easy to be in love with the awen (inspiration) and to ignore the heroic virtues. Throughout my long life, I have seen both, and I give as much credence to the one as to the other. Indeed, when all is said, they are not so very dissimilar. The warrior fights tangible enemies with a sword and buckler; the poet fights darkness and ignorance with words and song. A poem concerning a hero is a magical invocation requiring courage as well as inspiration. In the end, both heroic deeds and the poems sung about them are acts of power. ❧ I will tell now of a poet, one whom I loved and respected as much as any man, who lived by the code of the warrior, but whose vision stretched beyond that of any hero I have known. His name was Aneurin, and his story, and the story of the great elegy he composed, is one of the shining fragments of the history of these Islands. ❧ Listen well, then, little monk, and you shall hear a story of stories, of the bravery of men, and the love of men, and the pity of men. I, Taliesin of skillful speech, tell it as it occurred, in the name of the Cauldron and the Wood. ❧ Mynyddog was Lord of Dun Eidyn[1] and the Cantref of Gododdin.[2]

He was a wealthy man and proud of his descent from the kings of the Island of the Mighty. His lands lay between the Merin Iddew and the Tyneand, bordered on one side by the lands of Ystrad Glud, that are nowadays called Strathclyde, and by Lothian and the great kingdom of Dalriada in the north. Southward lay the lands of Bernicia, home of the Saeson barbarian Ina, who styled himself a king in his own place, but was known only as "The Dark One" among the folk of the Gododdin.

Each year in the raiding season, Ina's men crossed the borders into Gododdin and plundered the rich lands they found there. Gradually they grew more and more bold, once even striking to within a day's march of Dun Eidyn itself. Mynyddog was angry enough about this, but when he heard that Ina's neighbor, Osric of Deira, was looking to join forces with Ina the following year, he grew alarmed. "If both the Bernicians and the men of Deira attack us, we may well be overwhelmed," he said. "Let us therefore raise an army of our finest warriors and take the war to them."

And so, Mynyddog sent forth the word to every warrior in his lands to assemble at Dun Eidyn for the feast of Beltaine and promised to feast them all for a year. This was no small undertaking, but Mynyddog was a wealthy man. As word of his desire spread, the men came, in ones, twos, and threes, until almost three hundred filled to overflowing the halls and outbuildings of the Dun. For a year, Mynyddog entertained them royally, armed them with new weapons where they required it, trained them, and feasted them nightly. They say that nearly a thousand gallons of mead were drunk in the halls of Dun Eidyn in that time, and that five hundred sheep and as many cattle were killed to feed the bellies of the three hundred.

Aneurin had come to the court of Mynyddog from Ystrad Fawr, where I had first met him among the circle of initiates around the Cauldron's rim.[3] He had none of the desire to wander that affects many who drink from that vessel. Perhaps, unlike mine, his vision was of a more personal kind. At least, he seemed always like one in pursuit of a dream that he could never quite catch. Or, it may be that he had found what he sought at Dun Eidyn, and for that reason he never moved on from there. For on the day that he entered Mynyddog's hall, he saw Teleri for the first time.

Aneurin was the son of Dwydai, daughter of Lleynnog and Dunod Fawr. Thus he had the right to call himself one of the Coeling, the great family descended from Coel Hen or Coel Godebog, which made him a prince in his own right.[4] He was a gentle man, more handsome in my sight than either Ancelot or Trystan. Women fell at his feet like ripe plums, but he seemed scarcely to notice them—until Teleri, that is.

Teleri's hair was as dark as a cloud from which the sun, her radiant face, looked out. She had a way of walking that made his heart feel light. From the moment Anuerin saw her, he was lost. But, Teleri was the wife of Ufri—little, dark Ufri who thought her the best prize he had ever won, though he had no use for her delicate ways and love of singing. Theirs was no love match. Teleri's father had arranged the marriage, took the bride price, and gave Teleri to Ufri with as little thought as he would to the bartering of cattle. Because she was a dutiful girl, Teleri suffered the attentions of her husband, when he was not too drunk to notice her, cleaned and cooked and kept house for him like a bondwoman. She was as faithful to Ufri as a woman could be—until she saw Aneurin, after which everything changed.

To be sure, they scarcely spoke to each other, except in the way of things, when they passed in the hall or encountered each other about the Dun. Only Aneurin noticed the way she changed color when he was near, how she avoided meeting his eyes and seemed always to wear her best clothes whenever she was going to be in his company.

For his part, Aneurin took to seeking the company of Ufri and his brother Heidyn,[5] who were both much flattered by the attentions of the poet who was looked upon with awe as one of the Cauldron-Born. They could not have known that Aneurin was befriending them so that he could spend more time in the presence of Teleri, even if he had little chance to speak with her.

As these events were unfolding, the year of preparation was passing. Soon, it was time for Mynyddog's warband to set forth. Mynyddog himself provided horses so that the entire troop could be mounted. As they rode away from Dun Eidyn, pennons fluttering in the wind, horses stepping proudly, sunlight flashing on helmet and spear point, the three hundred were a stirring and noble sight. Among them rode Aneurin, who bore the title "Prince of Poets" or was called "Aneurin of the Flowing Verse."

They rode, until they came to the place called Catraeth, where they met the forces of Bernicia and Deira, who outnumbered them ten to one. The battle lasted four days, with truces to collect and count the dead on both sides. Many heroes fell that day, the sunlight dying in their eyes. Aneurin lists them all in his famous elegy: Eithin and Erf, who fought like bulls; Gwefrfawr, who seemed a veritable wolf in his fury; Cynon, who lay in wait for the enemy like a serpent; Beli and Cadfannan, who were as eagles in the fray. The list is a long one. How should it not be, since almost all the three hundred warriors of Dun Eidyn perished in that battle?

Almost, but not quite all. Aneurin escaped, as did Gwawrddur, Tafloyw, and Heidyn. But among those who would not come again to the lands of the Gododdin was Ufri, husband of the woman Teleri, whom Aneurin loved. It is their story I would tell now, though the very thought of it lies heavily upon me. For though the destruction of the warband at Catraeth is a litany of death, yet the warriors fell as warriors always wish to fall, fighting alongside their companions, with the hero light in their eyes. But the death of Aneurin was another matter.

News of the battle reached Dun Eidyn on a bleak day more than a month after the warband had departed. Mynyddog wept openly, and everywhere women keened for their dead and the dead of Gododdin. "What now will prevent the Saeson from overwhelming us?" was the cry that rose from every throat. Mynyddog sent messages pleading for assistance to Lot of Lothian, Urien of Rheged, and even to Uther far off in the south.[6] But even as he did so, he knew that it could only be a matter of time before the Saeson struck further north. He set about preparing what defenses he could, though they were inadequate, since all able-bodied warriors had ridden out with the warband.

Slowly, painfully, the survivors of Catraeth returned. In all, five men, all wounded. Among them were Aneurin, who despite the sacredness of his person as a Bard, had fought along with the rest and received a deep sword wound in the thigh, and Heidyn, brother of Ufri, who had suffered a blow to the head, which carried away his ear and left the sight of one eye blurred. Since Heidyn was unmarried and her dead husband's brother, Teleri took him in and nursed him, along with Aneurin, who had been her husband's friend.

It must have been in those long and painful weeks that Teleri and Aneurin became lovers in earnest. And it must have been then that Heidyn came to know of it, for there is little that can be hidden from men who have shared such deep and terrible times.

As the weeks passed and no more men returned, the story of what happened at Catraeth began to emerge from the scarred memories of the survivors. It became clear that the men of the Gododdin had sold their lives dearly, but that the losses to the Saeson had been terrible also. The enemy would not come raiding north that year, though in the next season, they would find little or no opposition.

Meanwhile, under the care of Teleri, Aneurin began to mend. The wound in his leg healed and the terrible days at Catraeth could be faced. He began to think of the song that he would sing in praise of those who fell in the great battle. Heidyn did not heal so surely. It became clear that the blow to his head had done more damage than was seen at first. He lay for days in Teleri's hut, neither moving nor speaking, though his good eye followed the movements of his brother's wife around the room with feverish intensity. With time, the wounds to his head and face began to heal, and he grew stronger, yet there was something about him that seemed unchancy, and he spoke not at all of the battle.

Throughout the dark days of autumn, Aneurin worked on his song about Catraeth. At last the day came when he declared himself ready to sing it before the court. That song is, perhaps, the finest I ever heard, certainly the greatest elegy of any made for the warriors of the Island of the Mighty. I pray that it has been written down and that the writing survives these dark days—darker, even, that those in which it was written.

I *have heard that the great song of the Gododdin was indeed set down by one who heard it recited long after the death of the poet.*

That night, in the hall of Mynyddog, there were none who did not weep to hear again the names of their fallen comrades, husbands, and sons. The old lord himself cast his cloak across his eyes and was silent. When at last the song was ended—and a while it took to sing all the names and deeds of the warband—Mynyddog gave Aneurin two great gold arm rings and a golden torque thick enough to have belonged to a chieftain. For though the men of the Gododdin had fallen, yet had they been remembered by as great a poet as ever sang in the hall of kings.

Yet one man neither wept nor rejoiced to hear the song of Catraeth. Heidyn sat silent and morose throughout the singing; and when Aneurin was done, he rose and left the hall without speaking to anyone. But he must already have known, in the part of his mind that was not dead, what he intended—indeed, he must have been planning it for some time.

Aneurin left the hall and returned to his own hut, for now that he was healed, it was not right for him to remain in the house of his friend's wife. Indeed, it would be long months before he could approach her openly with an offer of marriage.

On the next day, he did not appear, and many thought he was sleeping more deeply than usual after the great singing of the night before. But as night fell, and Aneurin had still not appeared, Teleri went to his hut and found it empty. Then it was noticed that Heidyn was also missing, and that no one could recall seeing him since the previous night. A search was made of the Dun, for there were many empty places since Catraeth, but no sign was found of either the warrior or the poet. Then folk began to think and to wonder, and they remembered things about Teleri and the poet that they had seen without understanding.

The search widened, but without result. Then, a shepherd boy found by chance that the entrance to one of the old grave mounds had been disturbed and thought he heard one of his charges crying out within. Being braver than most, he struggled to move a great stone that had been half-pulled across the entrance and crawled within. What he found there sent him flying back to Dun Eidyn with a white face and trembling body. Scarcely able to speak, he guided others to the place where the work of Heidyn was revealed. Aneurin's body had been hacked to pieces with an axe and mutilated horribly. His harp lay broken by his side, and his blood had soaked into the earth. Of Heidyn there was no sign, nor was his body ever recovered. It was assumed that he had wandered off in his madness and pain and died in the hills to the north. As for Teleri, the blow of Aneurin's death left her without will or strength. She died that same winter, carried off by a chill she no longer cared enough to fight.

Thus died Aneurin, the Prince of Poets, without good reason and to no good end. His remains were laid to rest with due ceremony, though none were present to sing his praise song. He is mourned still among those of the Cauldron and the Wood, who remember the brightness of his star and the words he sang concerning the warband of Gododdin. I have remembered his songs and learned to sing them myself. How could I not, for on the night he died, I dreamed of him, laughing in the sun as I had known him as Ystrad Fawr and heard him sing these words which you will not hear when the tale of Catraeth is recited:

> *Taliesin, I made this song for you,*
> *In the presence of all the court.*
> *A home for maggots, I do not seek vengeance,*
> *Stretched out in this earthen cell.*
> *I, yet not I, sing of Gododdin—*
> *Let Aneurin be remembered in Taliesin's song.*

AT THE WEIR AGAIN

Sunlight stretched tight over rock,
Rock scraping the skull, the tongue,
The poet's hands; the shock
Of light recalling songs sung.

Gray water smooth between reaches
Where pale winds rattle reeds at the bank;
He who learned what the dream teaches
Laughed as the bright flame sank.

19
THE VOYAGE TO ANNWN

here is a story I must tell that I have struggled not to tell. It is the story of Arthur's voyage to Annwn, and it used to be told everywhere in the Land. In more recent times, another tale has taken its place, telling how the Ymerawdwr and his warriors raided Annwn to bring back the Cauldron of Plenty. That story is almost completely untrue. There are other, darker things hidden within it, things that have little to do with the actions of heroes. I shall tell the real story now, as it truly happened, and so speak at last of a bargain struck between the Ymerawdwr and the Lord of Annwn, which was to have a far-reaching effect upon all that happened thereafter. ❧ It begins one time when Arthur was at Carlisle, where the Wood washes up almost to the walls, stopping only a league or so distant, as though it wanted to overwhelm the great city but thought better of it. There it was that I told, by the light of the flickering torches, the old tale of Blessed Bran and of his Cauldron that could bring the dead back to life, though without speech, so that they could not tell what they had seen beyond the gates of death. ❧ As I told the tale, I saw how the King leaned forward in his

chair, eyes gleaming with a light that was, perhaps, no more than the reflection of the torches, but which I saw more truly as emanating from the depths of his soul.

In the weeks that followed, Arthur became increasingly remote, dealing as ever with matters of state, but seeming to have little interest in other things. I knew that it was only a matter of time before we came to hear what it was that occupied his mind.

At last he called his closest advisers, including myself, and spoke his thoughts aloud. "It is my wish," he said, "to make a journey. It will be a dangerous one, and I will ask only those who desire it to accompany me."

We all looked at one another, wondering what this presaged. At length, as so often, it was I who spoke up. "To what place would you journey, my lord?"

Arthur smiled openly. "Why, to Annwn," he said, and at that naming, there was not a man present who did not feel a cold mote of fear strike him. For Annwn was the country of Arawn, the dark lord who hunted the lands above and beneath with his pack of red-eared, white-bodied hounds. None living had ever entered his abode and returned to tell of it, save only Pwyll who, it was said, had once exchanged places with Arawn and served as king in that land for a year.[1]

"Why would you go there?" asked another of the advisers in wonderment, fear writ large upon his face.

"I seek the Cauldron that Bran the Blessed once owned, of which our noble Bard Taliesin spoke but recently. It is well known that after the death of Bran, when the Feasting of the Noble Head was over, the Cauldron was carried into the lands beneath and given into the keeping of Arawn himself. There it rests still, and there I would journey to discover it."

The royal counselors were silent for a time. Then, for whatever reason, something made me laugh aloud. "Why not, indeed? I, for one, will go." I do not know why I said this, and to this day my heart turns over when I think of it. Yet I must believe, for otherwise my mind would crack, that there was a deeper purpose.

Some of the reasons for it I have begun to understand, but there is much that remains hidden, even from me.

Thus it was that, after due preparation, when the next new moon rose above the Island of the Mighty, Arthur set sail in his ship Prydwen, accompanied by a crew of thirty men, the best, it was said, of the warriors of the Island, and including myself.

It seems strange, now, that we simply set forth, with no real idea of where we were going. But things were different then, and we were willing to dare anything for our lord. It was known that the entrance to Annwn lay somewhere beyond the northernmost edge of the Land, and so we sailed north, blindly following the certainty that drove Arthur onward like a wolf at his back.

Two weeks of rough weather and wild water brought us at last to a place where the sea became suddenly still. The wind dropped, and Prydwen's sails hung empty. The crew broke out the oars and began to row forward steadily; though there were none there, save Arthur and myself, who did not look over his shoulder as he went, for the air of that place became steadily thicker, until it was difficult to breathe, and a darkness more tangible than night deepened around us.

How long we continued in this manner none could say, for time itself has no meaning in that place. But at length I cried aloud from where I sat in the prow, keeping watch for them all. As all looked where I looked, they saw, far off, like a star in that lightless place, a gleam.

Scarcely moving now, so intense was the darkness and so thick the air, the ship sailed on, driven by slow deep strokes of the oars. And as she went, gradually the darkness began to lift, until it was possible to see something of our surroundings.

Around us the water lay flat and black as a mirror with nothing but darkness to reflect, all the way to the feet of a great outcrop of rock, which rose sheer into the sky for a hundred leagues or more. The light we had seen came from here, and by its bleak radiance we saw that we were in a natural inlet, surrounded by walls and towers, pinnacles and turrets, of black, adamantine stone. Leading to that towering edifice was a path of water, flanked by six vast pillars smaller than those that hemmed us in.

A light dawned in the King's eyes, almost as fierce as that which burned far above us. He gave the order to move forward, and though there was not a man who cared to do so, yet all answered to their lord's will and pushed the ship onward towards the towers of Annwn.

When no more than a league separated us from the frowning cliffs, the water ahead began to boil, as though the inlet were itself a great Cauldron. As we looked, there rose from the midst of the sea a huge and terrible head. Serried ranks of teeth gleamed in a mouth large enough to swallow Prydwen with ease. Two great luminous eyes glared down upon us, as the head rose higher and higher into the air, carried on a huge and gleaming neck.

Men cried out in fear, and Arthur drew Caledflwch that in more recent times has become known as Excalibur. Then the monstrous head drove in upon us, and when it lifted again, a third of Prydwen's crew were gone, swallowed by that dreadful maw. The air was filled with a high keening, whose source we could not see, but which echoed from the rocks on every side and was magnified a thousandfold.

Strange shapes danced in the air around the ship. Faces there were, seeming like long-drowned men, their flesh half-eaten or rotted away. Several of the crew leapt screaming over the side, to vanish forever into the darkly swirling tide. Prydwen leapt and wallowed and took in water until she was in danger of sinking entirely beneath the sea.

Then the creature rose again, its vast bulk cleaving the water, and its monstrous jaws gaping wide. Even Arthur's warriors, who had seen much that passes for strange and terrible in the world of men, cowered in the sculls, holding their weapons above them in a vain hope of fending off the dread creature. I, too, felt fear, yet something moved me to a strange response. From where I stood at the bow of the ship, I raised my voice in a chant. The words were foreign even to me, being in a tongue more ancient than that of men, yet I found them in a deep place within me and uttered them with all the strength I possessed.

Their effect upon the monster was immediate. Its eyes and mouth closed, and it gave vent to a bellow that rocked the ship and set men to covering their ears. Then it rose high above us, its vast body showing almost entirely above the water. Streams of water crashed upon the deck of Prydwen, and mighty waves thundered against her sides, but as the monster sank again, the sea slowly settled back to its former calm.

Shaken, the men leaned upon their oars, as a great stillness fell once more around them. More than half the crew was gone; indeed, I counted only five remaining, six with the King. Then Arthur, murmuring his thanks to me, raised his head again to the tower that leaned above us. It was as though nothing, not even the loss of men, could come between him and his goal.

All followed his gaze and saw movement on the cliffs above. It was hard to see much in that dimly lit place, but it seemed that many hundreds of warriors stood there, all silent. Then one figure stood forth from the rest. Utterly dark it seemed, from its night-dark clothing to the black iron helm that masked its face. From within, carried easily on the air, came a cold voice. "Who would enter the Cauldron of Annwn?"

To which Arthur answered, "It is Arthur who comes, and with me the warriors of the Island of the Mighty."

Then was silence for a moment; then the voice came again. "Step up, little King, and let us talk awhile. But mind you, come alone. That other one is not welcome here."

Of course I knew that he meant me. I knew well in that moment that this was indeed Annwn's lord who stood before us. Arthur looked toward me with a question in his eyes. By way of answer, I made mocking obeisance to Arawn.

By skillful use of oars and rudder, Prydwen was guided close to the base of the great rock, and there Arthur leaped lightly ashore. Scrambling, not without difficulty, on the slippery surface, he climbed swiftly to where the lone figure waited. They spoke for a while, and none knew what passed between them.

The warriors fingered their swords uneasily, ready if need be to leap ashore after their lord and defend him to the last, while I gripped the forepost of my harp as though I would crush it.

Soon we saw the King returning and brought the ship close enough for him to leap aboard. He seemed pale and shaken and went straight to sit alone in the center of the ship. None there were who wished to speak with him, or to ask what had passed between him and the Lord of Annwn. Everyone waited in silence until Arthur gave the order to put away from the dreadful rock and back towards the center of the inlet.

There the King ordered the warriors to cease rowing and to look down into the water. "Behold," he said, "the Cauldron of Annwn, on which we are permitted to gaze by its master. Let no one forget what he has seen today, for this is a great mystery." We obeyed with no little fear, wondering what more terrors that place held. What we saw has grown with the telling, and there are those who would dispute it. I can say only what I saw, who was there on that day.

Looking down into the depths, we saw that the water had grown clear, so clear that as we stood upon the decks of Prydwen, it seemed we were flying above a vast land with nothing between ourselves and it. Many cried out and clung to the sides of the ship for fear of falling. Below us lay what seemed to be a vast city, spread out upon the sea's base—a city with buildings and streets and houses, where men and women walked in the pallid light of great milky stones, which served as sun and moon in that place. It is said that those below looked up and smiled and raised their hands in greeting to those above, and that some among them were the warriors who had but lately fallen or been consumed by the great serpent.

Indeed, none would ever forget that place, or what they saw, for each one, it seemed, saw something there that was for him alone. One thing is beyond dispute: few words were spoken among the crew on the voyage back to the lands of the living.

After, when we had returned to the court, I made a song of these things, which is still sung in the Island of the Mighty.

Since my song resounded
In the turning Caer,
I am become preeminent.
My first song
Was of the Cauldron itself.
When we went with Arthur—a mighty labor
Save only seven, none returned from the Iron Caer

Since my song resounded
In the four-square city,
In the Island of the Strong Door.
Worth more am I than the clerks
Who see not Arthur's might.
Three shiploads of Prydwen went with Arthur—
Save only seven, none returned from the Cauldron's Rim.

Beneath Caer Siddi
The Light was dim and mixed with darkness.
Six thousand stood on its walls.
It was hard to speak with their leader.
Three shiploads went with Arthur—
Save only seven, none returned from the Caer of Darkness.

Of Caer Siddi I sing forever
This eternal invocation:
Save only seven, none returned
From the Cauldron of Annwn.[2]

And of Arthur himself? Who can say what passed between him and the Lord of Annwn? It is my belief that a dreadful bargain was struck between the Ymerawdwr and the Lord of Annwn, and that this was the true reason for the journey. Many such bargains were made at this time, and after, a terrible price had to be paid for them. The death of Arthur's only son Llacheu may well have resulted from a bargain I myself struck with the god Mabon—an act that will surely haunt me till the end of my life.[3]

There before the gates of Annwn, I believe that Arthur came truly to understand the reality of the task he had undertaken—to be the Guardian of the Island of the Mighty and to seek another vessel of life, the Grail, of which few had heard at that time. And I believe that, brave though he was, his heart quailed at the task.

If so, then the nature of the bargain is laid bare: that the Ymerawdwr pledged to give up his chance at love and family in order to find the strength to rule over the Land.

Had I more clearly understood his intent I might have attempted to dissuade him from his course, though few there were who might do so, once his mind was made up. That I failed in this may well be one of the most terrible wrongs I own, though I pray it may not be so.

From that moment, it seems to me, the fates of the Ymerawdwr and all who followed him—perhaps, of the Land itself—were sealed. Soon Arthur would begin the great Quest for the thing known as the Grail, which would sow the seeds of destruction among the Fellowship of the Round Table. Gwenhwyfar, his Queen, was, perhaps, already lost to him, her heart given to Ancelot—the Lady of the Lake's bright gift.

Thus we went to Annwn to reave back the Cauldron and instead brought back something else—a terrible power that flooded through the Land and drove the Ymerawdwr to become the greatest ruler of this or any age. Yet I do not think, when all is said and done, that we got the best of the bargain. In the end it was Arawn who won, though his victory was an empty one since he could not prevent Arthur from returning to Avalon. There, I continue to believe, he remains, the lord I followed for so long; and from there he will one day return, to trace his star across the heavens as he did in our own time.

From this I take what comfort I may, knowing that we are each caught up in the implacable tide of life.

My master's words are a puzzle to me here. There is a grimness about his final words that haunts me. Throughout the Land there have been stories of a mystery that surrounds the passing of the Lord Arthur: that he did not in fact die, but went instead to the place that my master names Avalon, an island, it is said, that is always temperate, and that lies between this world and that Other to which he so often referred. From here, the rumors have it, he will one day return, when he is needed.

I am but a simple man, who has come to these things through circumstance, and as such, I do my utmost to remain detached. Yet I cannot help but reflect that it has been my lot to see through the windows of my master's eyes into a world that passed me by, but which in truth touched me more deeply than I knew, as it did all who dwell in the Island of the Mighty.

THE KING'S MOON-RITE

From the mounds of Crooked Bank there came but three common men:
Morvran mab Tegid, who for his ugliness no man would strike;
Sendaf Bright Angel, who for his beauty
death forefend; and Glewlwyd Mighty Grasp,
whose strength none might withstand.

And these three through the field walked arm-in-arm
as Logres-in-Britain crumbled into darkness again,
and dreams rode in the Land because
of the one who struck the Grievous Blow
(the Red Man from the Lake);
of he who forbore to ask the question;
of the Ship of Glass that never sailed
but rode the shape of Bardsey while the Bear
went out in Prydwen to rifle Hell
to come again with gifts for all who still held true.

He it is who is remembered in the stars—
Arcturus and Telyn Idris—nor do the mountains forget
the debt of Crooked Bank.
But the Head of Bran no longer stares above Lud's Town,
Nor is it known who lay in need: King Pellam,
Lord of Lystenesse, or the Crow with Singing Head?
But she who waits beyond the water, watching all,
crooning to her poet-lover, caught within the bush,
who saw her floating on the water's moonlit silver
that has not also heard her siren song?
And who has seen the Cup flame in the west
that has not also seen the breath of Nine

smoke on the air to warm the Cauldron's rim?
And who has seen the Table that has not also seen it crack
as men rode over it with plunging hooves of steel
to scatter the titled chairs in which the Hosts had sat?

The Sword went down in water, shaken and drowned.
The Sword was named Escalibor; the Spear, Rhongommyniad;
The Mantle of Brightness, Gwern.
But he who was both King and Dux, Director of Toil, Ymerawdwr,
Lord of the Wave in ancestral purple, walking in the Waste,
sits yet upon his golden chair, his hair and beard grown long,
And leads the Hounds of Annwn over the height of moor and peak.
And in the caves he sleeps, the Bear, the Crow, the Saturnine Lord,
and casts a silver horseshoe on Saint John's Eve,
and guards the Burning Tree for better days.

20

THE DOORWAY TO THE SUMMER STARS

hree times I have been in the prison of Arianhrod. The first time was when I drank the draught of the Cauldron; the second, when I entered the heart of the Wood in search of Llacheu. But the third time—ah, that was a different matter! Three times in these past nights I have dreamed of that third visit. I believe that these visions are a sign to me that my work here is almost complete. I shall, therefore, write of that final visit and place my telling where it will not be easily found, for I am of a mind that it contains matters that ought not to be seen by ordinary men. Yet I will set them down, nonetheless, for reasons that I only half-understand, with the knowledge that this account is, perhaps, the last thing I shall write.

I believe my master to have spoken the truth, and that these are, indeed, his last recorded words. His long task complete, his great chronicle written, and the tales he had told to me done as well, there seemed no reason for him to remain. Also, perhaps, there was other work

that called him. These are mysteries too great for me to speak of, but I continue to offer prayers to Lord Christ daily that my master shall find rest when it is his time, and that I, if I am spared, may bring together more of the tales he left behind in my care, which treat more directly of the Ymerawdwr.

In my vision, I stood on a hillside, from which I could see a field of standing corn, still green, still growing. The wind fled across it, combing patterns through it, parting it like hair. I began to walk, not knowing where I went, nor why I was there, yet feeling that I must go on. Then, before me on the grassy plain, there came a shimmer of light that hardened into a door, half open, through which I glimpsed a night sky filled with stars. I walked towards it unafraid. As I did, the door opened wider. I stood upon the sill, staring out at the stars. Before me rose a crystal stair. I set one foot upon it, then another. Suddenly I was running up the stairs and into the heavens themselves. I felt like an excited child. On every side the great dark pall of the sky stretched, and on its surface the stars flamed.

I grew dizzy, climbing. But there before me suddenly was another door, set in the midst of the heavens. I went through it into what seemed a great hall, greater than any I had ever entered. Vast pillars stalked proudly upon either side; the roof was lost in darkness. The floor on which I stepped seemed of crystal; through it I could see stars, scattered below me. On either side, between the pillars, more stars winked in iridescent chains like bubbles in a stream of pure water. I felt, as I have felt before, part of everything, of the whole of creation, as though I had been somehow divided into a million tiny pieces and scattered throughout the place where the stars dwell.

Then I saw where the hall ended. There was a great mirror, large enough to reflect worlds in its depths, set in a frame of living, silver trees, greater than any that ever grew on earth. I looked within the mirror, expecting to see myself reflected there. But there was only a milky swirl of stars, as though this were indeed a window upon another place. Then I saw, coming from far away, a shining figure,

THE DOORWAY TO THE SUMMER STARS

who wore seven stars on her brow, and whose raiment glimmered with the light of stars. Very fair she was and terrible.

Between the frame of the living trees she stopped and looked at me. I knew at once in whose presence I stood. I had seen her before, though always far off, from the first time I drank of the Cauldron, to the time when I had walked the secret ways of the Wood, with Merlin at first, then later alone. I remembered a day when I had stood close by a still pool and sought within its depths the presence of the Salmon of Wisdom.

"There," I seemed to hear a voice beside me say. "Look down, further, further. See where he swims, in a lake of stars."

I looked, as I had done a thousand times before, and saw, tiny and clear, a shining circle of starlight, where the great fish swam. But not only the Salmon was there. Another moved within the pool, one whose presence had been with me always, though I had never truly acknowledged her before. Then, I had turned away, left the Wood for a while, and lived again in the world of men. Now, when I fled no longer, I beheld her clearly and felt the power of her presence.

Words were spoken between us then that affirmed me in the service of the Wood. And from her I learned, also, much that I had not understood before, despite all my wisdom. For she had held the reins all along. Though I had never been a puppet—freedom is affirmed in everything that has its being in the world— yet I had ever been half-aware of those guiding hands.

It grows late, now, and the shadows are lengthening. I must hasten to the end. For how long did I stand before the goddess of stars? It may have been a moment, or maybe part of me stands there still, listening to the voice in my mind, learning how the spirals of the Wood form a pattern beyond my understanding. Somehow, I found my feet upon the stair again, while around me the stars sang words to which my very soul responded, as if it were natural to hear the heavens filled with the voice of creation. Then the door was before me again, and through it the same plain of wind-harried corn and the green hillside.

I did not look back. I knew the door was no longer there, in the same way that I know that it will open for me again when the time comes—perhaps not long from now—and that I shall be allowed to sojourn there again for a while.

For three nights I have walked in the region of the Summer Stars and listened to the voice of Arianhrod,[1] she whom I have always served, though I have almost never acknowledged it. All the words I have written, all the truths I have told, seem now to have been made under her tutelage. They remain as my testimony to the deeds of my Lord Arthur and those who followed where he led. In the days since his passing, I have learned that there is no end to this telling and that it will continue long after my own words have turned to dust.

I have come to believe, also, that there is a mystery in the stars that I have yet to plumb. In the shapes and patternings I have followed all my days, and which I have almost, though never wholly, understood, I have glimpsed another pattern, one that is still beyond my understanding, but which yet seems, at times, more familiar than all the rest.

That, I will seek.

TALIESIN'S SONG OF THE APOTHEOSIS OF BRITAIN

I am the owl whose blood
Drained through the earth
Where the Stone of Grownw fell,
Shivered by a single spear.
I am the raven who saw
The towers of Caer Siddi fall,
Who watched the smoke curl up
From Druid fires on Wansdyke Hill.
Last, I am the poet-sage
Who saw the Age of Man arrive,
And danced on Glastonbury's winter hill
As the Serpent slid from view;
Who saw the warrior Michael fall,
And heard the Dragon singing to its hoard.

In moonlight I gave witness
to the rites of Arthur's passing in the barge;
And sang the ancient stones to rest
Amid the clanging echoes of Craig Ddhu—
Watching all the while, in misted dawn

The slow sad birth of day
From Silbury's burning hill.

Now I have come to rest at last,
And stretch forth my hand to grasp
The sleeping Giant's staff;
While in Merlin's grove, the head of Bran
Sings Caer Siddi into silvered dust,
And moonlight stains the ancient ways
That lead to the Dragon's eye.
The White Horse of the downs gets up,
And goes to meet the mourning Queen,
Whose dreams become my truth again
As night rolls back before new day.

SOURCES

M̳ost of the stories in this collection belong to the main stream of Celtic myth and folklore. They have many resonances with The Mabinogion, versions of which are listed below. Also listed here is a selection of books that will enable the reader who wishes to do so to go deeper into the themes and patterns revealed in these texts.

PRIMARY SOURCES

The Mabinogion. Edited and translated by P. K. Ford. Berkeley: University of California Press, 1977.

The Mabinogion. A new translation by T. P. Ellis and John Lloyd. Oxford: The Clarendon Press, 1929.

The Mabinogion. Edited and translated by Lady Charlotte Guest. London: J. M. Dent, 1937 and various reprints.

Triodd Ynys Prydein (The Welsh Triads). Edited and translated by Rachel Bromwich. 2d ed. Cardiff: University of Wales Press, 1988.

STUDIES

Darrah, John. *The Real Camelot.* London: Thames & Hudson, 1981.

Jones, David. *The Anathemata.* London: Faber & Faber, 1952.

———. *The Sleeping Lord.* London: Faber & Faber, 1981.

Markale, Jean. *King Arthur, King of Kings.* Rochester, Vt.: Inner Traditions, 1998.

———. *Women of the Celts.* Rochester, Vt.: Inner Traditions, 1997.

———. *Celtic Civilization.* Rochester, Vt.: Inner Traditions, 1999.

Matthews, Caitlín. *Elements of the Celtic Tradition.* Shaftsbury, Dorset: Element Books, 1989.

———. *Mabon and the Mysteries of Britain.* London and New York: Penguin Arkana, 1987.

———. *Arthur and the Sovereignty of Britain.* London and New York: Penguin Arkana, 1989.

Matthews, John. *Taliesin: Shamanism and the Bardic Mysteries in Britain and Ireland.* London: Unwin Hyman, 1990. 2d ed. Rochester Vt.: Inner Traditions, 2001.

———. *Fionn MacCumhail.* Poole, Dorset: Firebird Books, 1988.

Matthews, John, and Caitlín Matthews. *The Arthurian Book of Days.* London: Sidgewick & Jackson, 1990.

———. *The Arthurian Tarot.* London: Thorsons, 1990.

———. *Hallowquest.* London: Thorsons, 1990.

Ross, Ann. *Pagan Celtic Britain.* London: Thames & Hudson, 1967.

SOURCES FOR INDIVIDUAL STORIES

"The Journey to Deganwy"

Barber, Chris. *Mysterious Wales.* London: David & Charles, 1982.

———. *More Mysterious Wales.* London: David & Charles, 1986.

Gildas. *The Ruin of Britain.* Chichester, Sussex: Phillimore & Co., 1978.

Lloyd, J. E. *A History of Wales.* London: Golden Grove Editions, 1989.

Morris, John. *The Age of Arthur.* London: Weidenfeld & Nicolson, 1973.

Wood, Juliet. "Maelgwn Gwynedd: A Forgotten Welsh Hero." *Trivium*, vol. 19 (1984): 103-107.

"Ogma: The Search for the Letters"

Macalister, R. A. S. *The Secret Languages of Ireland.* St. Helier/Amsterdam: Amoricer Book Co./Philo Press, 1956

Meroney, H. "Irish Letter Names." *Speculum* XXIV (1955-6): 19-43.

"The Salmon and the Crane"

Meyer, K. "The Boyish Exploits of Finn." *Eriu* 1 (1904): 180-190.

Nagy, J. F. *The Wisdom of the Outlaw.* Berkeley: University of California Press, 1985.

"Iskander and the Show-Stone"

Haycock, M. "Some Talk of Alexander and Some of Hercules: Three Early Medieval Poems from the Book of Taliesin." *Cambridge Medieval Celtic Studies*, no.13 (Summer, 1987): 7-38.

Pseudo-Callisthenes. *The Romance of Alexander the Great.* Translated from the Armenian by A. M. Wolohojian. New York: Columbia University Press, 1969.

"The Battle of the Trees"

Graves, Robert. *The White Goddess.* London: Faber & Faber, 1952.

The Myvyrian Archaiology of Wales. Edited by O. Jones, E. Williams, and W. O. Pughe. Cardiff: Thomas Gere, 1870.

"The Inundation"

Lloyd, J. E. *A History of Wales.* London: Golden Grove Editions, 1989.

North, F. J. *Sunken Cities.* Cardiff: University of Wales Press, 1957.

"Amairgen's Story"

Rhys, J. *Lectures on the Origin and Growth of Religion as Illustrated by Celtic Heathendom.* London: Williams & Norgate, 1888.

"The Crow, the Salmon, and the Oldest of the Old"

Hyde, Douglas. *Legends of Saints and Sinners.* London: T. Fisher Unwin, 1915.

Hull, Eleanor. "The Hawk Of Achill, or the Legend of the Oldest Animals." *Folk-Lore*, vol. 43 (1932): 336-409.

"The Fall of the Great Trees"

Best, R. I. "Settling of the Manor of Tara." *Eriu*, vol. 4 (1912): 121-172.

Byrne, Francis John. *Irish Kings and High Kings.* London: Batsford, 1973.

Dillon, M. "Stories from the Law Tracts." *Eriu*, vol. 11 (1932): 154-165.

Dillon, M. "The Yew of the Disputing Sons." *Eriu,* vol. 14 (1946): 154-165.

Gwynn, E. J. *The Metrical Dindshencas.* 5 vols. *Todd Lecture Series* 8-12. Dublin: Gill, 1903-1935.

Lucas, A. T. "The Sacred Trees of Ireland." *Journal of the Cork Historical and Archaeological Society* 69 (1964): 16-54.

Watson, A. "The King, the Poet, and the Sacred Tree." *Etudes Celtiques,* vol. 18 (1981): 165-180.

"The Hunting of Hen Wen"

Barber, Richard. *The Figure of Arthur.* London: Longman, 1972.

Bromwich, Rachel. *Trioedd Ynys Prydein.* 2d ed. Cardiff: University of Wales Press, 1978.

"The Death of Aneurin"

Aneirin. *Y Gododdin.* Translated and edited by A. O. H. Jarman. Cardiff: The Welsh Classics, 1988.

Ford, P. K. "The Death of Aneirin." *Bulletin of the Board of Celtic Studies,* vol. 34 (1987): 41-50.

"The Voyage To Annwn"

Loomis, R. S. *Celtic Myths and Arthurian Romance.* New York: AMS, 1987.

Matthews, John. *Sources of the Grail.* Hudson, N.Y.: Lindisfarne Press, 1998.

———. *Taliesin: Shamanism and the Bardic Mysteries in Britain and Ireland.* London: Thorsons, 1991. 2d ed. Rochester Vt.: Inner Traditions, 2001.

———. *King Arthur and the Grail Quest.* London: Cassell, 1988.

NOTES

𝕿he notes left by the Scribe are often in themselves unclear, since he was writing for a different audience than that of today. These additional notes are therefore provided to help readers find their way through the complexities of the text and to establish where possible the relationship of Taliesin's writings to previously existent texts. These notes are indicated in the text by superscript numbers.

INTRODUCTION

1. Originally published (London: Harper Collins, 1991). Republished (Rochester, Vt.: Inner Traditions, 2001).

1: THE SCRIBE'S STORY

1. The phrase "a heap of all I can find" reappears in the ninth-century writings, known as the *Historia Brittonum,* by the monk Nennius.

2: THE CAULDRON-BORN

1. It is evident that what is being described here is a shamanic initiation rite of the kind I have discussed at length in *Taliesin: Shamanism and the Bardic Mysteries in Britain and Ireland* (see Sources). In this rite, the initiate was taken to a sacred place, probably a cave on the side of a mountain or another high place. Here would have stood a carved stone of some kind, bearing certain symbols on which he would meditate, having been also perhaps given a drink containing a drug that caused him to be freed from an everyday state of consciousness. Taliesin's vision is clearly the root of his life history. A variant version can be read in Lady Charlotte Guest's translation of *The Mabinogion* (see Sources).

3: THE JOURNEY TO DEGANWY

1. A version of this story will be found in Lady Guest's *Mabinogion*. Essentially, some time after his initiation on the Sacred Mountain, Taliesin appeared at the court of Gwyddno Garanhir and became tutor to his son Elffin, whose luck was considered to be so abysmal that the most fortunate event of his life was the discovery of Taliesin, washed

ashore in the salmon weir on the strand of the River Conway. In a later story in the collection, "The Inundation," Taliesin hints again at the nature of his coming.

2. See "The Inundation," pp. 117-127.

3. According to the legends of the time, Afallach was a powerful lord of the Otherworld, which was believed to exist alongside the mundane world and to overlap with it at times. It is thus by no means unusual to read of marriages or other dealings between men and immortals. Afallach sired a line that was to include Ygrain, the mother of Arthur, and Morgain "the Fay," whose opposition to her half-brother is chronicled in many other texts. The Daughters of Afallach became so famous that some scholars have deemed them a school of priestesses rather than the actual progeny of any single sire.

4. Llacheu (pronounced Thlackai), only son of Arthur and Gwenhewfar, met his death under strange circumstances while seeking the White Beast that the Goddess of the Land sent periodically to Camelot to test and challenge the fellowship of the Round Table.

5. One of the most famous historical Bards of the time. None of his works have survived, but he is mentioned in several ancient texts including the Triads of Britain.

6. This refers to the idea, expressed in the writings of medieval authors, such as Geoffrey of Monmouth (*Historia Regum Brittaniae*), that Britain's royal house was descended from Brutus, grandson of Aeneas of Troy who, fleeing from his home, found his way to the shores of Britain. I have written more on this subject in my chapter "New Troy: London Before History" in *The Aquarian Guide to Legendary London*, ed. John Matthews and Chesca Potter (London: Thorsons, 1990).

7. These refer to archaic verse forms, which a fully trained Bard of the court was expected to know. In attacking thus at the very foundation of Hennin's knowledge, Taliesin insults him deeply.

8. It is believed that the Bards and shamans of Britain preserved a more ancient tongue no longer spoken save by them, and that this was a kind of Speech of Initiates that could only be understood by those who had undergone the training and trials of the Bardic Schools. In some texts it is called "the Dark Speech."

4: OGMA: THE SEARCH FOR THE LETTERS

1. The Ogam alphabet is one of the great wonders of the Celtic world. Essentially, it consists of a series of strokes cut against or across a straight line or "stave." Each of the letters thus formed possessed a vast number of symbolic references. Thus, the letter "B" or "beith" could refer to a tree, an elder, or a door. All of these associations were learned by heart by the Bards.

   Of Ogma, its legendary originator, little is known, though his epithets "Sun-Face" and "Honey-Mouth" suggest that he may have been a sun god. His other name "The Strong Man" has prompted some scholars to suggest an identification with the great hero Herakles, whose shadow seems to have reached even to Celtic lands. In some texts, as here, Ogma is also called a god of poetry.

   Ogam itself has remained something of a mystery, as have its uses, although there are known to have included the magical and the mystical. In recent years, commentators such as Robert Graves have identified each letter with a tree or shrub and have suggested that Ogam represents a kind of callendrical system practiced by the Celtic Bards and shamen. For further information, see Robert Graves, *The White Goddess* (London: Faber & Faber, 1952) and my *Taliesin: Shamanism and the Bardic Mysteries in Britain and Ireland*, especially chapter 8.

2. Taranis, also known as "The Thunderer," was the Celtic god of the Wheel, associated with human fate as well as storms. He is, perhaps, akin to the Norse god Thor.

3. The Tuatha de Danaan were the tutelary gods of Ireland, after the Fomorians, whom they overthrew. Lugh is Lugh Longhand, the god of light and truth; Goibnu is the god of smiths; Macha and Morrigan are goddesses of war and death; Eriu is the personification of Ireland herself, whose appearance could be fair or hideous at will. Bran is the wounded god, whose story appears later in "The Entertainment of the Noble Head," pp. 71-81.

4. The Washer at the Ford is the dreadful figure seen on the eve of battle by warriors. She washes their bloody shirts as a forewarning of their imminent deaths.

5. This story actually appears in a classical text by the Roman writer Lucius. In Welsh, Hercules becomes Ercwf and appears in more than one of the still extant poems by Taliesin, suggesting another link of association between the Celtic god and the Greek hero. For a further discussion of this association, see my *Taliesin: Shamanism and the Bardic Mysteries in Britain and Ireland*, chapter 8.

6. Mag Mell is one of several Irish names for a region of the Otherworld.

7. This image is strongly reminiscent of Nechtan's Well, which is mentioned several times in Irish mythology. If anyone with evil in his/her heart looked into it, he/she was blinded by the light that came from within it.

8. Thus, almost by accident, we learn the origin of the great forest mentioned again and again in Celtic mythology and legend, frequently by Taliesin himself. The exact nature or site of the forest remains elusive, however, though the remains of it can be seen today in Brittany.

5: THE SALMON AND THE CRANE

1. Finn or Fionn is Fionn Mac Cumhail, the greatest warrior and hero of Ireland. He has been identified with, or compared to, Gwion Bach by several commentators, since their names derive from a common root.

2. Logres is one of the ancient mystical names for Britain. In Arthur's day it seems to have stood for the inner realm of which he was guardian and Merlin the progenitor.

3. Taliesin's, or Fionn's, experiences are typical of shamanic initiations in every part of the world.

4. Possibly Taliesin is hinting at a mystery here. Finnecus, the old man, is in some way connected to the salmon itself, which is sometimes named Fintan. The epithet *Finn* (white) seems to possess the connotation of wisdom.

5. According to Robert Graves in his essay "The Crane Bag" in *The Crane Bag and Other Disputed Subjects* (London: Cassell, 1965), these objects gave rise to a set of "extra" letters in the Ogam alphabet. See also the chapter on Ogam in my *Taliesin: Shamanism and the Bardic Mysteries in Britain and Ireland.*

6: THE ENTERTAINMENT OF THE NOBLE HEAD

1. This story is found in a significantly different version in *The Mabinogion*, though Taliesin is listed there as one of the seven who escaped from Ireland after Bran's expedition to recover the Cauldron and set right the wrong done to his sister.

2. The "Story of Taliesin," as found in *The Mabinogion*, tells that the Cauldron, from

which Taliesin drank when the three drops splashed upon his finger, was prepared by Ceridwen, the ancient Welsh goddess of inspiration. After Taliesin's rebirth as her son, we hear no more of this strange family.

3. The Sovereignty of the Land is a concept that appears frequently in both Irish and Welsh mythology. Essentially, it describes the gifting of the Sovereignty of the country to its King by a mysterious Otherworldly woman who is, in effect, an embodiment of the Land itself, seen as sacred in the person of the goddess. For a detailed discussion of this tradition, see two books by Caitlín Matthews, *Mabon and the Mysteries of Britain* (London and New York: Arkana, 1988) and *Arthur and the Sovereignty of Britain* (London and New York: Arkana, 1989) in which many of the themes of this story are explored.

4. This curious custom is mentioned in several early Irish texts. The precise reason for it is uncertain, but it is clearly related to the totemic nature of the pig.

5. The Welsh family of gods known by this name are a close equivalent to the Children of Danu in Irish myth. Thus we may perceive that Bran the Blessed is the same as the figure mentioned in the story "Ogma and the Search for the Letters."

7: CULHWCH'S DAY

1. A very different version of this story appears in *The Mabinogion*.

2. The Triads are a collection of mnemonic verses once used by Bards and storytellers as a way of remembering the countless stories they must learn. Unfortunately, we now possess only a few of these. They have been brilliantly edited by Rachel Bromwich as *Trioedd Ynys Prydein* (Cardiff: University of Wales Press, 1969).

3. This poem is a translation of one of a number of works attributed to Myrddyn Emrys, the bardic incarnation of Merlin.

4. These characters appear in *The Mabinogion* story of Culhwch and Olwen in a somewhat different version to that given here.

5. The custom of requesting the cutting of hair by the king or lord of a hall is an ancient one. References to it are found in Celtic myth and in the stories of other lands. It is a totemic action relating to the transference of power and marks the coming of age into manhood. Culhwch shows his knowledge of arcane lore by this request.

6. There are three great Boar Hunts recorded in Celtic mythology: the hunt for Hen Wen,

a pig of Otherworldly qualities who gave birth to a number of strange offspring and whose story is told in this collection; the hunt for Twrch Trwyth which is recorded in the Welsh Triads; and the hunt described here. The pig and the boar were sacred beasts to the Celts, and in the case of Twrch Trwyth, the fact of Arthur's hunting it was more than a symbolic act. It was one the many tests devised by the Otherworld guardians of the land through which he earned the right to be High King of Britain.

7. In the story of Geraint ab Erbin, also found in *The Mabinogion*, the hero's quest for the woman Enide who, as has been demonstrated by Caitlín Matthews in her book *Arthur and the Sovereignty of Britain*, is another of the many images of Sovereignty to appear in the Arthurian cycle.

8. The reference here is clearly to the Quest for the Holy Grail, the cup believed to have been used by Christ to celebrate the Last Supper and the first Eucharist. In later, medieval stories, it is Galahad, son of Lancelot who achieves this quest.

8: ISKANDER AND THE SHOW-STONE

1. There are several references in Taliesin's poetry to the figure of Alexander the Great. In the famous poem that he sang before Maelgwn Gwynedd (see pp. 42-43), he refers to having "carried the banner before Alexander," a curious statement we may consider either as a poetic truth, or in the light of Taliesin's own explanation as a further example of his ability to be present at more than one time and place.

2. This poem is my own adaptation of an original attributed to Taliesin himself.

9: THE BATTLE OF THE TREES

1. The original version of this story is known from two conflicting and fragmentary sources: the poem "Cad Goddeu" (Battle of the Trees) from the Book of Taliesin and a cryptic reference in the nineteenth-century collection known as *The Myvyrian Archaiology of Wales*, O. Jones, E. Williams, W. O. Pugh, eds. (Cardiff: Thomas Gere, 1870). For an alternative theory regarding this story, see Robert Graves, *The White Goddess*.

2. The story of Arawn and Pwyll is told in the first branch of *The Mabinogion*. A detailed discussion of this story is found in Caitlín Matthews, *Mabon and the Mysteries of Britain*.

3. The Celts had no concept of Hell such as we find in the Christian teachings. The

---

Otherworld was a place that held many terrors, as well as wonders, but it was by no means a dark place, nor were those who dwelled there necessarily dead. Gods and goddesses, Otherworld folk of all kinds, enchanted beasts and enchanted humans were all to be found there.

4. In making my own version of this poem, attributed to Taliesin, I followed the edition by J. Gwenogvryn Evans (Llanbedrog: privately printed, 1915). The original text, with a less accurate translation, can be found in *The Four Ancient Books of Wales* by W. F. Skene, reprinted (New York: AMS Press, 1984-5). The poem is discussed in full in my own *Taliesin: Shamanism and the Bardic Mysteries in Britain and Ireland* and is also retranslated there.

10: THE INUNDATION

1. The story of this terrible inundation is well documented, though the reasons for it have remained a matter for speculation. Archaeological evidence points to an area of Cardigan Bay being covered by the sea at a date near to the time we can assume to be referred to here (c. sixth century AD), while local legend tells stories of drowned bells heard beneath the sea on stormy nights, sometimes heralding new disasters.

11: AMAIRGEN'S STORY

1. This story is referred to in *The Book of Leinster*, ed. R. Atkinson (Dublin, 1880), though there are substantial differences in this version.

2. The two great smith gods of the Celtic and Anglo-Saxon peoples. Goibhniu was responsible for forging many famous weapons for the Irish heroes; Wayland, called "the Smith of the Gods," is still remembered at Wayland's Smithy in Oxfordshire.

3. The parallels between the training of the shaman and the poet were considerable. Both underwent a rigorous program lasting several years, and both were able to perform magical acts of great power. This parallel is explored further in my *Taliesin: Shamanism and the Bardic Mysteries in Britain and Ireland*.

4. This is almost certainly a reference to Ogam, the mysterious symbolic system of writing that enabled poets skilled in its use to converse with each other in secret and without the knowledge of others who might be present.

5. The parallels that Taliesin notes are of some interest. The links between the inspired shaman-poets of the Celtic world are notable. The references to "cooking" and watching over a Cauldron may imply the brewing of a sacred initiatory drink.

6. These phrases appear in a similar form in "The Colloquy of the Ancients," an Irish text that deals with a lengthy exchange of wisdom between poets. A full translation of this text appears in my *Bardic Source Book* (London: Cassell, 1998).

12: THE CONTENTION OF LLUD AND LLEVELYS

1. Another variant of the story found in *The Mabinogion*. Various folktales support Taliesin's version, though many of the details of his telling are unique to his vision.

2. The kin of Arthur, from Uther onwards, took the name Pendragon, which is to say "Chief Dragon" and suggests an identification with the Dragon Power believed to lie just beneath the surface of the Land. The name may also be a title that dates from far earlier times in the mythic era before Arthur came to power.

3. For the full story of this later event, see Geoffrey of Monmouth's *History of the Kings of Britain* (Harmondsworth: Penguin Classics, 1966) and the commentary in *Mabon and the Mysteries of Britain* by Caitlín Matthews (London: Arkana, 1987).

13: THE CROW, THE SALMON, AND THE OLDEST OF THE OLD

1. A variant version of the ancient tale that follows is found in *Legends of Saints and Sinners*, collected and translated by Douglas Hyde (London: T. Fisher Unwin, 1915). It belongs to a type of story known as "The Oldest Animals," found in the folklore of many countries.

2. This refers to an old Irish legend that says that two of the sons of Noah escaped from the ark and traveled to Ireland, where they settled and founded colonies that became absorbed into the native people.

3. Gol, the one-eyed salmon, also appears in the marvelous text known as "The Hawk of Achill." A full translation of this piece, together with a discussion of the symbolism of the Oldest Animals theme, appears in my *Taliesin* and in the forthcoming *Celtic Totem Animals* (London: Connections Book Publishing, 2001).

4. The various peoples listed here are all described in *The Book of Invasions* as leading various waves of incomers to the land of Ireland. Fintan is the name of the ancient Salmon of Wisdom who appears in "The Salmon and the Crane" as the source of Fionn's wisdom.

5. The Druid's Wisp is mentioned in several early texts. It was apparently woven from certain grasses, and when cast over the person whom it was intended to affect, could bring madness. Taliesin's interpretation differs slightly from those in Irish texts.

6. This tantalizing reference is clearly to a story, no longer extant, which told of a continuing opposition between Ceridwen and Tegid Foel, who is here presented as a wizard similar to the more famous Gwydion mentioned elsewhere in these stories. The mysterious connection between Ceridwen and Tegid, who in later texts is euphemistically referred to as her "husband," suggests an ancient primal rivalry of the kind attributed to Greek deities like Zeus and Hera.

7. Several versions of this famous old rhyme have been preserved. The reference to the Alder Pole in lines 2-3 probably refers to the shamanistic idea of a central pole upholding the sky. Compare, for example, the information contained in the story "The Fall of the Great Trees," pp. 151-159.

14: THE FALL OF THE GREAT TREES

1. The concept of the World Tree is familiar from Norse myth, where Ygdrasil is described in similar terms. In shamanic literature, the concept of the tree that the shaman climbs in order to present his visionary insights is encountered in many parts of the world. This story speculates on a Celtic version of this mythic pattern.

2. The Three Worlds referred to here are sometimes named as Abred, Ceugant, and Annwn, though the first two seem to have no history beyond the eighteenth-century forgeries of Iolo Morgannwg, edited by T. Williams (Llandovery: William Rees, 1948). See the discussion of the Iolo ms. in my *Taliesin and the Bardic Mysteries in Britain and Ireland*. However, the concept of the division of the universe into three levels, above, middle, and below, is common to most shamanic cosmologies.

3. This theme is taken up again and elaborated in the story here titled "The Defense of the Chair," pp. 169-176.

4. Referred to in detail in "Ogma: The Search for the Letters," pp. 51-59.

5. This custom is well documented in Irish literature, where the power of the poets is clearly recognized. From evidence assembled by recent scholarship, it seems that the Sacred Trees were very much a part of the inauguration ceremony of the Kings of Ireland.

6. The trees listed here are all to be found mentioned in ancient Irish texts such as the *Dindsenchas* or the *Senchus Mor*. For a more detailed discussion, see my *Taliesin and the Bardic Mysteries in Britain and Ireland* and refer to the list of source reading in the present book.

7. See "The Salmon and the Crane," pp. 61-68.

8. We are here in mythic time, before even the most ancient chronicles of Irish proto-history were compiled.

9. Trefuilngid Treochair is referred to in the text of "The Settling of the Manor of Tara" (see Sources), where he has something of the status of a god. Even the writer of the text seems uncertain whether to portray him as an angelic being or a pagan god. His name means, literally, "Upholder of the Sky," suggesting a distinct and ancient cosmological significance.

10. As there are only three fruits mentioned as growing on the branch, how did five trees grow from them? We must assume that two pairs of trees were of the same genus, such as two apple trees, two oaks, and one hazel, or some such combination.

11. *The Book of the Invasions* survived and may still be read today. It describes the succeeding waves of conquerors who annexed Ireland for themselves. It is no longer easy to distinguish mythical from actual peoples.

12. This may be a reference to a kind of geomantic, earth wisdom, in which the pattern described by the falling trees marked out a sacred enclosure, the purpose of which is no longer understood. The very careful noting of the direction in which each tree fell seems significant, however, and may well be related to divinatory practices.

13. A very similar poem is to be found in the *Dindsenchas* ascribed to the Tree of Ross. The epithets express the sacred nature of the Tree, its connection with the High King, and its undoubted magical properties.

14. The whole story of the Quest for the Grail and the Cauldron is described in many medieval texts relating to Arthur. See my *Sources of the Grail* (Hudson, N.Y.: Lindisfarne Press, 1998) for a selection of the best of these.

15: THE HUNTING OF HEN WEN

1. Cai is one of the oldest recorded warriors of Arthur. His name appears in the earliest texts, always as a figure of heroic stature. It was only later that he achieved the reputation of being a braggart and boaster. The Antor referred to here is probably the same as Ector of later Arthurian romances, who appears as the father of Cai and Arthur's foster-father.

2. See "Culhwch's Day," pp. 83-95.

3. This story is told partially in "Culhwch and Olwen" in *The Mabinogion*.

4. This is probably the Bristol Channel. The great Celticist Sir John Rhys gives a detailed account of the route taken by Hen Wen in his *Celtic Folk-Lore: Welsh & Manx* (London: Wildwood House, 1975).

5. This is evidently a kind of cosmological myth, of which the Celts were clearly fond. It is no longer possible to say with any certainty what is being referred to here; however, Taliesin's comments are of interest. The transmission of symbolism and the nature of Celtic cosmology is dealt with at length in my *Taliesin*.

6. This part of the story is no longer extant, but we may assume that the wolf and the eagle brought more trouble than good to the princes of Arfon.

7. The idea that there was a kind of "cold war" between Arthur and the Otherworld is commented upon by Jean Markale in his book *King Arthur, King of Kings* (see Sources). Certainly it is an interesting way of explaining the frequent visits of Otherworldly characters to the Arthurian court, usually with spectacular results.

8. The legends of the Cath Palug are referred to several times in Celtic and later Arthurian myth. The principal reference is in Welsh Triad 15, which tells of Hen Wen and her offspring.

9. A fuller version of this song has survived. It is usually referred to as "Pa Gur" and tells of a series of magical encounters involving the heroes of Arthur's warband, including Cai. This story offers an interesting insight into this rather neglected character. For a fuller discussion, see Linda M. Gowans, *Cei and the Arthurian Legend* (Woodbridge, Suffolk: Boydell & Brewer, 1988).

16: THE DEFENSE OF THE CHAIR

1. Annwn is one of the many names of the Celtic Otherworld. It has associations with the quest for the Cauldron of Inspiration and Plenty described in Taliesin's most famous poem "The Raid on Annwn,"which appears in this collection, pp. 141-142. The poem is discussed in full in my *Taliesin and Bardic Mysteries in Britain and Ireland*.

2. Taliesin seems to speak here of the shamanic technique of the visionary journey, in which, after entering an altered state of consciousness, the shaman "travels" in a way scarcely understandable to the modern mind.

3. The story of Cormac's visit to the Otherworld is well known and may be summarized as follows: Cormac received an invitation to enter the Otherworld, where he was severely tested by the folk who dwell there. Having succeeded in all that he was given to do, he received as a reward a four-sided cup, the properties of which were that if three false-hoods were declared in its presence, it broke into three pieces; but that if three truths were then spoken in its presence, it became whole again. In one version of the story, Cormac receives the cup from an Otherworldly woman who is clearly a type of Lady Sovereignty. This leads us to the conclusion that the person Taliesin encountered who held the Chair of Prydein (an ancient name for Britain) in her gift, was the goddess of Sovereignty herself, who empowers kings and bestows the Guardianship of the Land.

4. This chronology establishes the time of the story fairly certainly to be between the departure of Merlin and the beginning of the Quest for the Grail, which, as the scribe rightly assumes, is being referred to here.

17: THE PROTECTION OF THE HONEY ISLE

1. The figure of Sovereignty is discussed in detail in Caitlín Matthews, *Arthur and the Sovereignty of Britain*. Briefly, this Goddess represents the spirit of the Land itself, and her relationship to the King is all important. In Irish mythology putative kings underwent a form of mystical marriage with Eriu, the Sovereignty of Ireland, before they could be recognized as chosen rulers.

2. Sometimes we catch a glimpse of an almost Atlantean race of beings behind the screen of Taliesin's words. At other times, he seems to identify these ancient wise ones with the Sidhe, the god-like people who dwelled in the Hollow Hills of Britain and Ireland, perhaps the last vestiges of a proud race, or an almost forgotten family of goddesses and gods, once worshipped by the indigenous people of the British isles.

3. The Lake is that magical place beneath which the Lady who fostered Ancelot (Lancelot) had her dwelling. In the *Morte D'Arthur* by Sir Thomas Malory and elsewhere, the Lady of the Lake is responsible for providing Arthur with his famous magical sword Excalibur (Cut-Steel), of which she is also the Guardian.

4. This story is told in fragmentary form in "Culhwch and Olwen" in *The Mabinogion*. For a detailed discussion of the meaning of this story, see Caitlín Matthews, *Mabon and the Mysteries of Britain*.

5. A stone bearing this name still stands to this day in Dumfriesshire. Whether it was this to which Taliesin refers is only conjecture.

18: THE DEATH OF ANEURIN

1. Edinburgh.

2. Gododdin was one of the richest cantrefs in Britain from the middle of the sixth to the early seventh centuries, when it was overrun by the Saxons. Its story is told, in words attributed to Aneurin, in the great heroic elegy that also bears the title "The Gododdin." The most recent and best translation is by A. H. O. Jarman. (See Sources for full reference.)

3. Apparently the site of bardic/initiatic college where Taliesin learned his art. In later years a Christian monastery was sited there.

4. He is so named in Welsh genealogical tracts. King Coel, who founded one of the greatest of the old British dynasties, is probably the "Old King Cole" of the nursery rhyme.

5. Both these warriors are named in the text of "The Gododdin."

6. The mention of Uther indicates that the events described took place before the time of Arthur.

19: THE VOYAGE TO ANNWN

1. See "Culhwch's Day," pp. 83-95.

2. This poem is based upon one long attributed to Taliesin titled "The Spoils of Annwn," which may be the oldest surviving account of the Grail Quest. A full commentary on this poem can be found in my *Taliesin and the Bardic Mysteries in Britain and Ireland*.

The version used there differs in some details from the account within this story.

3. As told in the story titled "The Protection of the Honey Isle," pp. 179-188.

20: THE DOORWAY TO THE SUMMER STARS

1. Arianhrod is considered among the Celts to be the goddess of the starry heavens. It seems wholly appropriate that she acted as Taliesin's inner guide or muse.

QUEST BOOKS
are published by
The Theosophical Society in America,
Wheaton, Illinois 60189-0270,
a branch of a world fellowship,
a membership organization
dedicated to the promotion of the unity of
humanity and the encouragement of the study of
religion, philosophy, and science, to the end that
we may better understand ourselves and our place in
the universe. The Society stands for complete
freedom of individual search and belief.
For further information about its activities,
write, call 1-800-669-1571, e-mail olcott@theosmail.net,
or consult its Web page: http://www.theosophical.org

The Theosophical Publishing House
is aided by the generous support of
THE KERN FOUNDATION,
a trust established by Herbert A. Kern
and dedicated to Theosophical education.